FORMOSA

THE BROOKINGS INSTITUTION

The Brookings Institution is an independent organization engaged in research and education in the social sciences. Its principal purposes are to aid in the development of sound public policies and to provide advanced training for students in the social sciences.

The Institution was founded December 8, 1927 and was the outgrowth of three antecedent organizations: the Institute for Government Research, 1916; the Institute of Economics, 1922; and the Robert Brookings Graduate School of Economics and Government, 1924.

The general administration of the Institution is the responsibility of a self-perpetuating Board of Trustees. In addition to this general responsibility the By-Laws provide that, "It is the function of the Trustees to make possible the conduct of scientific research and publication, under the most favorable conditions, and to safeguard the independence of the research staff in the pursuit of their studies and in the publication of the results of such studies. It is not a part of their function to determine, control, or influence the conduct of particular investigations or the conclusions reached." The immediate direction of the policies, program, and staff of the Institution is vested in the President, who is assisted by an advisory council, chosen from the professional staff of the Institution.

The Institution in publishing a study presents it as a competent treatment of a subject worthy of public consideration. In such publications the author, or authors, have freedom to present their final interpretations and conclusions, although these may not necessarily be concurred in by other members of the staff or by the administrative officers of the Institution.

FORMOSA

A Problem for
United States Foreign Policy

By
JOSEPH W. BALLANTINE

THE BROOKINGS INSTITUTION
WASHINGTON, D.C.
1952

Foreword

IN 1946 the Brookings Institution inaugurated a program of research and education in the field of international relations, which was an expansion of the earlier efforts of the Institution in the international field and was based on a policy of continuing investigation of problems having a direct bearing on the national interests of the United States. The main emphasis was placed on a study of the current American foreign policies. The general approach was and continues to be the analysis and interpretation of the developments in world affairs that give rise to problems of policy for the Government of the United States.

In undertaking the program, the Institution has two primary objectives: to aid in the development of an informed and responsible American public opinion on foreign policy; and to contribute toward a more realistic training of the increasing number of American specialists in international relations that are required today in the Government, in business, and in other agencies operating abroad. The Institution seeks to contribute to the achievement of these objectives by providing in its publications a type of analysis of major problems of United States foreign policy that is not usually found in specialized textbooks and general treatises on the subject, and by arranging conferences designed to stimulate discussion based on this type of analysis.

For the execution of this program, the Institution has organized a part of its staff into an International Studies Group, composed of specialists in various fields of international relations in general and of United States foreign policy in particular. The Group, which is directed by Leo Pasvolsky, is engaged in a series of investigations on major developments in the field of foreign affairs as they bear on the foreign policy of the United States. The results of these studies are made available in the form of books and pamphlets. The following titles have been issued to date: *The United States and the Restoration of World Trade, Governmental Mechanism for the Conduct of United States Foreign Relations, The Security of the Middle East, Anglo-American Economic Relations, The Search for Peace Settlements, Current Issues in Foreign Economic Assistance,* and *Rearmament and Anglo-American Economic Relations.*

In addition, the Group prepares an annual analytical survey of the major problems of United States foreign policy. It has also conducted, in various parts of the country, seminars and other conferences for teachers of international relations.

This volume on *Formosa* is a further study of the International Studies Group. The author, Joseph W. Ballantine, is especially qualified to write on this subject. He was an officer of the American Foreign Service from 1909 to 1946 and was stationed at different times in Formosa and elsewhere in the Far East. He served as Director of the Office of Far Eastern Affairs in the Department of State in 1944-1945, and as Special Assistant to the Secretary of State in 1945-1947, before joining the staff of the Brookings Institution.

The scope of the Institution's program of international studies is made possible by special grants of funds from the Rockefeller Foundation, the Carnegie Corporation of New York, and other foundations, which supplement the Institution's own resources available for this purpose. Grateful acknowledgment is made of the assistance generously given by these foundations.

ROBERT D. CALKINS
President

Director's Preface

UNTIL three years ago, the island of Formosa was of little concern to the United States or to the world at large. For several centuries prior to the Sino-Japanese War of 1895, it was an integral part of China. Thereafter, for fifty years it was a colony of Japan. At the conclusion of the Second World War, it reverted to China.

Late in 1949, however, the island suddenly acquired a world-wide importance and came within the sphere of active interest of the United States. This happened when the National Government of China, defeated on the mainland by the Chinese Communists, followed the precedent of the defeated Ming dynasty of three centuries earlier and took refuge in Formosa. As a result of this and other far-reaching developments in the Far East, the fortunes and the future status of the island became inextricably enmeshed with the problems of the United States in relation to China as a whole, to Korea, to Japan, to the Far East in general, and to global power relationships.

At the present moment, the problem of Formosa is relatively quiescent. The urgency of finding a satisfactory solution has been temporarily relieved by the neutralization of the island by the American Navy and by the fact that American public attention is fixed on the critical situation in Korea. But the problem has by no means been solved. The unresolved elements in it can become pressing at any time and in many ways.

The present study has been prepared with this possibility in mind. Its purpose is to acquaint the reader with the position in which the United States now stands with respect to Formosa and with the facts and considerations pertinent to forming judgments on ways and means that may need to be taken into account in dealing with the problem of Formosa.

The study begins with a description of the physical setting of the island and an account of its political and diplomatic history, with emphasis on the administrative, social, economic, and military policies and developments of the several regimes that ruled the island, one after another, until the National Government of China retreated there in 1949. This is followed by a brief review of the political developments in China that resulted in the withdrawal of the National Government from the mainland; an analysis of the policy of the United States toward Formosa and of the nature and extent of American aid to it; and an examination of the problem of Formosa in relation to the United Nations and the Japanese peace treaty. The study concludes with an estimate of the present position of the United States with respect to Formosa and a review of the principal unresolved questions as regards the future.

In the preparation of the study, the author has had the benefit of valuable criticism and advice from Stanley K. Hornbeck, George H. Blakeslee, and several other specialists on Far Eastern affairs. He alone is responsible for the accuracy of the factual material, for the views expressed, and the conclusions reached in the book.

Leo Pasvolsky
Director
International Studies Group

November 15, 1952

Contents

CHAPTER 10

APPENDIXES

PART ONE

THE BACKGROUND

CHAPTER 1.

The Land and the People

THE ISLAND of Formosa, which the Chinese and the Japanese call Taiwan, is a link in a chain of islands stretching from Kamchatka to the Malay Peninsula and sheltering the coastline of the East Asian mainland from the open Pacific. Formosa is parallel to the mainland of China and is separated therefrom by the Formosa Straits, which are 90 miles wide at the narrowest point. It extends from north-northeast to south-southwest with an extreme length of 243 miles, a breadth generally ranging from 60 to 80 miles, and an area of nearly 14,000 square miles—approximately equal to that of Massachusetts, Rhode Island, and Connecticut combined. Lying between Japan and the Philippines, the most northeasterly point of Formosa is about 350 miles west by south of Okinawa, and its southernmost tip is 225 miles north of Luzon. Due eastward, the nearest land is Iwo Jima, some 1,000 miles distant; and southeastward, 1,500 miles away, lies Guam. In the Straits, about 25 miles from the coast of Formosa, is a cluster of low-lying, storm-swept islets, the Pescadores. These islands historically have been a political appendage of Formosa. With an aggregate area of 25 square miles, they are important only because of their strategic position. The Japanese during their occupation maintained a naval station there.

About two-thirds of Formosa is mountainous, and 42 per cent of the entire surface is of an elevation exceeding 500 meters (1,640 feet). Parallel mountain ranges run longitudinally along the eastern part of the island, reaching their highest elevations in Mt. Morrison,[1] 13,075 feet, and Mt. Sylvia, 12,972 feet. Seventy-seven other summits of the central range approximate or exceed a height of 10,000 feet. The eastern part of the island is generally too rugged for extensive cultivation. Most of the cultivated land, which in 1940 was 2.1 million acres or 23 per cent of the total area, lies along the western slopes and in the coastal plain stretching toward the Straits.

Formosa has a coastline of more than 1,000 miles. Characteristic features of the west coast are wide, dune-covered beaches and long stretches of mud flats exposed to tidal changes. The sea is so shallow that sea-going vessels have to keep almost out of sight of land and can find ingress only at a few river mouths. These approaches, moreover, are often choked with sand bars. On the east coast, while depths permit ships to come in close to shore, the mountains are a barrier to penetration inland. Formosa has only three natural harbors: Keelung, in the north, formed by a deep indentation in the coast and protected except from direct north winds; Suao, in the northeast, which is somewhat remote from the main centers of population; and Kaohsiung in the southwest, where the harbor is formed by a long lagoon. The Tamsui River is navigable for small junks as far as the capital, Taipei, 12 miles inland. The rivers are generally short, swift, and subject to seasonal floods. Con-

---

[1] In the present text, the accepted European name will generally be used when there is one. When there is no Europan name, the Chinese name will generally be given. For explanation and glossary of Formosan geographical names see Appendix.

sequently, they have wide beds, which make them difficult to bridge. The configuration of the coast and the
topography of the land facilitate the defense of the island against external invasion by sea.

Formosa is bisected by the Tropic of Cancer, and the
climate at sea level is tropical or semitropical. At the
higher elevations it is temperate. The climate is significantly affected by the southwest monsoon, which blows
from May until September; by the northeast monsoon,
prevalent from November until April; and by the Japan
("Black") current, which flows from the south and
divides, passing both the east and the west coasts of the
island. The North has most of its sunny days in the summer, and the South in the winter. February can be as
raw in Taipei as in places several degrees farther north
on the eastern seaboard of the United States, while
Tainan, only 200 miles farther south, is at that season
generally balmy. Rainfall decreases from north to south
and from east to west.

Forests cover about two thirds of Formosa. At the
higher elevations and in the north the giant cryptomeria,
spruce, hemlock, pine, and Mongolian oak are among
the most valuable timber trees. The island has been the
world's principal source of natural camphor. At the
lower altitudes the forests assume a tropical character.
Giant bamboos abound in the foothills, and groves of
them are found beside nearly every village. The western
coastal plain and the piedmont region are well suited
for diversified agriculture. The slopes yield Oolong tea
and pineapples. With an abundance of water, the lowlands are adapted to the growing of rice and sugar,
as well as of ordinary vegetables and tropical fruits. The
seas around the island teem with edible fish and shell-
fish. So far, proven mineral resources are not abundant.

The most valuable are coal and gold. A more thorough
exploration of the wild eastern section may yield
further discoveries. Another resource probably capable
of substantial further development is water power.

Ethnographically, Formosa is roughly divided into
longitudal strips corresponding to the topographical
divisions. A major lowlands strip capping the head of
the island in the north and following the line of the
foothills to the southern tip, together with a narrow
lowland strip paralleling the east coast between the central massif and the coast range, are densely populated
by peoples of Chinese origin. A major highland strip
along the central massif and a minor highland strip
along the east coast range are sparsely inhabited by primitive aborigines.

The Chinese settlers have come for the most part
from the neighboring mainland provinces of Fukien and
Kwangtung. The Hoklos from Fukien speak principally
the Amoy dialect of Chinese and are noted for their conservatism; in Formosa, the women bound their feet and
the men wore pigtails for years after China had, under
the Republic, abandoned those fashions. This stock has
furnished perhaps three fourths of the Chinese population of the island.

The Hakkas, numbering perhaps a million, are descendants of immigrants from farther north in China,
who settled first in eastern Kwangtung Province and
then spread from there not only to Formosa but also to
sparsely populated areas in the mainland of south China
and to Hainan Island. They speak a dialect intermediate
between northern and southern Chinese speech. On the
mainland of China, the Hakkas were among the most
enthusiastic supporters of Sun Yat-sen's republican revolution and gave the National Government some of its

best soldiers. Most of the Hakkas in Formosa moved early from the coast to the areas bordering the domain of the aborigines, and there has been some intermarriage between these stocks. The Hakka women never adopted the practice of foot-binding and, unlike the Hoklo women, have worked in the fields along with their menfolk. These people retain their vigorous individualism, as is evidenced, for example, by the fact that resistance to the Japanese occupation was bitterest in districts where Hakkas predominated.

A third Chinese group are the Cantonese, numbering perhaps 200,000, who settled principally in the south and are a merchant class. Since the Chinese reoccupation in 1945, there has been an influx from the mainland of about a million refugees many of whom are from north China and speak the standard national tongue.

The aborigines comprise eight groups of tribes. Mongoloid characteristics are dominant: high cheek bones, light brown skin, straight black hair, short stature and stocky frames; but most of them have straight rather than slanted eyes. In physical appearance many would pass, superficially at least, for Japanese, and others for Chinese. Both in physical appearance and in culture they resemble even more closely certain peoples of the islands to the south, especially the Dyaks of Borneo and the mountain tribes of northern Luzon.

Prior to the advent of the Chinese, the aborigines were essentially food gatherers and hunters, but they also engaged in rudimentary agriculture. Chickens and dogs were their only domestic animals. They lived in rude wooden or stone huts grouped in villages of 100 to 500 persons. Head-hunting was widespread, and was responsible for a chronic state of intertribal warfare. The majority of the aborigines still pursue a tribal and semi-

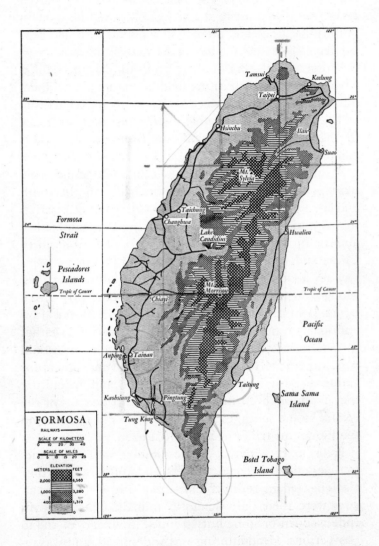

FORMOSA

RAILWAYS _____

SCALE OF KILOMETERS
0 10 20 30 40

SCALE OF MILES
0 5 10 15 20 25

ELEVATION
METERS   FEET
2,000   6,560
1,000   3,280
400   1,310
0   0

nomadic way of life. These are called *shengfan,* or "raw savages." A minority, known locally as *pepohuan* or "ripe" savages, have adopted a sedentary way of life, partially assimilated to the Chinese mode of life.

The population of Formosa in 1940 was placed at 6,077,385, of whom 5,523,912 (90.0 per cent) were domiciled Chinese, 346,663 (5.7 per cent) were Japanese, 158,321 (2.6 per cent) aborigines, and 48,489 (0.8 per cent) of other descents, mostly mainland Chinese. After the surrender of Japan in 1945, nearly all of the Japanese were repatriated. As a result of the influx of three times as many mainland Chinese and of natural increases, however, the total population had swelled by 1950 to more than seven million. In 1940, the mean density of population was 440 per square mile; but there was a great disparity between the eastern mountain area, where the average was 25 to the square mile, and the western lowland area (one third of the total) with 850 to the square mile.

It is not definitely known when Formosa was first peopled or whence its first inhabitants came. According to Chinese authorities there were migrations both from Luzon and from Malaysia. Chinese chroniclers record a few Chinese expeditions to Formosa between the seventh and fourteenth centuries, A.D., but these expeditions apparently made no effort to establish permanent settlements and left no definite impress.

It was not until late in the fifteenth century that Chinese settlers began to make their way into Formosa. It might seem surprising that until then the Chinese, whose expansion had spread far and wide even before the Christian era, had not earlier taken possession of this large and fertile island lying so close to the shores of China. The reason for the neglect of Formosa was

apparently the fact that early Chinese overseas settlement—in the Philippines and in Malaysia—normally followed trade, and in those days there was nothing in
Formosa to attract traders.

CHAPTER 2.

Formosa Under Chinese Rule

U NDER the Ming dynasty (1368-1644), especially before and after the close of the fifteenth century,
a combination of circumstances served to direct the attention of the Chinese to Formosa. For one thing,
Japanese pirates began to appear along the south China
coast and to commit depredations there. Many Chinese
who were disaffected with their own governments associated themselves with the Japanese pirates, who found
convenient stations in Formosa for their operations. The
Chinese authorities were powerless to put down the
pirates, and the depredations were extended until much
of the coastal area of south China was devastated. This
increased the distress of the inhabitants in parts of
Fukien and Kwangtung provinces, where pressure of
population upon the land was already becoming severe.
Many of the bolder spirits, especially among the Hakkas,
were prompted to seek relief and opportunity by moving
across the Straits to Formosa. Their numbers were augmented by fugitives from justice—and doubtless also by
fugitives from injustice. They landed for the most part
at points in the south and worked their way northward
and inland.

The Portuguese were the first Europeans to arrive
by sea in the Far East. In 1517 a Portuguese fleet under
Admiral Andrade appeared in Chinese waters. There is

no record, however, of the Portuguese having played a part in Formosa, although they called it "Ilha Formosa" —"the beautiful island."

Not until a century later, with the advent of the Dutch and the Spaniards, was there any attempt by Europeans to gain a foothold on the island. In 1622, 26 years after the Dutch had established themselves in Java, a Dutch fleet captured the Pescadores; and in the following year, the Dutch, by arrangement with the governor of Fukien Province, moved from the Pescadores to Formosa and founded in the southwest two settlements, Fort Zeelandia and Fort Providentia. Three years later, the Spaniards, who had established themselves in Manila in 1567, seized footholds in north Formosa at Keelung and at Tamsui.

Prior to the Nineteenth Century

At the time when the Europeans came on the scene, the Chinese settlers, who are believed to have numbered by then about 25,000, were engaged in a continuous struggle with the aborigines for land. There were also bitter rivalries and disputes between the Chinese and the Japanese. The troubles of the Chinese and of the Japanese were now augmented by the oppressive policies adopted by the Dutch in the course of their efforts to control trade. On one occasion there was a Chinese uprising, which the Dutch with the aid of 2,000 aborigines with whom they had established amicable relations, succeeded in putting down. There had been constant friction with the Dutch, and the Japanese withdrew from Formosa of their own accord in 1628. This withdrawal, however, may have been a consequence of the adoption by the Tokugawa Shogunate of a policy of national seclusion for Japan rather than of Dutch pressure. The Dutch found the presence of the Spaniards on Formosa detrimental to their trade, and in 1642, after an earlier unsuccessful attempt, succeeded in evicting them from the island.

After the Dutch had bested the Chinese, the Japanese, and the Spaniards, they eventually suffered reverses at the hands of a man of mixed Chinese and Japanese parentage, who had been known to the Chinese as Cheng Ch'eng-kung, to the Japanese as Teiseiko, and to Westerners as Koxinga. His father, Cheng Chi-lung, was a Fukienese who had started out in life as a tailor but had abandoned that calling for that of a petty trader. In the course of his travels, this trader spent some time in Macao, where he came under the influence of Catholic missionaries and was baptized; later at Nagasaki, he married a Japanese wife. Back again in China, he combined trade with piracy—to such advantage that he acquired a fleet of 3,000 vessels and amassed a fortune. In the struggle between the Mings and the Manchus, he used his resources and talents to oppose the Manchus. Eventually the Manchus entrapped him and led him away in chains to Peking.

Koxinga, his son, then carried on. Although still a mere youth, he was accepted by the Ming loyalists as their leader. He gained such favor with the head of the deposed dynasty that he was permitted to use the imperial family name, and he thus became known as Kuo Hsing-yeh (Kok Hsing-ya in the Amoy dialect). After a succession of brilliant victories by Koxinga's forces against the Manchus, victories attributed largely to naval superiority, the Peking (Manchu) Government, in 1660, despairing of prevailing against him otherwise, ordered the evacuation to the interior of all inhabitants within three leagues of the coast from the mouth of the Yangtze to Canton. Koxinga, thus deprived of his sources of supply, decided to transfer his headquarters from the Chinese mainland to Formosa and began preparations to that end.

The Dutch, forewarned of Koxinga's plans, urged their authorities in Java to send them reinforcements, but their pleas were not heeded. The slender Dutch garrisons at Fort Zeelandia and Fort Providentia, though better armed and better disciplined than the Chinese, were greatly outnumbered, for Koxinga's expeditionary force was augmented by islanders who flocked to his standards. The Dutch gave up Fort Providentia without a struggle, but held out in Fort Zeelandia for nine months. At the end of that time they were forced to capitulate, but on terms that were unusually liberal for those days. The Dutch governor, the remnants of the garrison, now reduced to 1,000, and the surviving Dutch civilians, except for a substantial number of hostages, were allowed to embark for Java with banners flying, with drums beating, and with muskets loaded, and to carry with them their records, their money, and such other property as they could move. In the following year a Dutch fleet, in an attempt to retake the island, captured Keelung but failed to extend the conquest. Two years later Keelung was abandoned as an unprofitable station. Thus ended the 38 years of Dutch rule in Formosa. The Dutch occupation left no significant impress, as Koxinga obliterated all traces of Dutch institutions and established a regime and institutions modeled on those prevailing in China.

Koxinga's ambitions next caused him to look to the Philippines as a field for conquest. He sent an emissary to Manila, an Italian Dominican friar whom he had known at Amoy, to demand that the Spanish governor pay an annual tribute and to intimate that in the event of noncompliance, the Philippines would be attacked. Although the emissary was received with befitting honors, the only result of the mission was a massacre by the Spaniards of large numbers of Chinese residents of Manila. Before Koxinga could complete his preparations for an armed expedition to the Philippines he died, at the age of 39 years. He was succeeded by his son Cheng Ching, under whose administration, as under that of his father, large numbers of Ming adherents from the mainland settled on the island and added to its prosperity. Unfortunately, the third Cheng exhausted his Ming forces on the Chinese mainland in vain efforts to drive out the Manchus. As a result, after his death in 1682 the Ming adherents in Formosa, then led by his son, the fourth Cheng, had not sufficient strength to resist effectively a Manchu expedition sent against them, and Formosa was absorbed into the empire of the Manchu dynasty.

Under the Manchus, Formosa was made a prefecture of the province of Fukien. The new administration retained as the island's capital city Taiwan (now Tainan), which Koxinga had established as the administrative seat, and thenceforth the name Taiwan was applied also to the whole island. There soon developed a marked deterioration in the efficiency of the administration, resulting partly from the Manchu practice of limiting to three years the tour of duty of officials. Application of this rule encouraged among the officials various practices of extortion, neglect of constructive measures for developing the well-being and prosperity of the people, and a general laxity in the discharge of official duties.

At the same time, the population of Formosa was more

turbulent than that of the mainland. This was natural in a new community, where frontier conditions prevailed, where no fixed patterns of life had been set, and where heterogenous social, cultural, and racial groups, only recently brought together, had not had time to become fused. Because of these facts and because there was still an undercurrent of loyalty to the deposed Ming dynasty, there were from time to time uprisings, widespread lawlessness, banditry and piracy, chronic inter-clan feuds, clashes between the Hakkas and the Pepohuans, and intermittent warfare between the Chinese and the wild tribes as the lands of the latter were encroached upon for camphor or for agricultural expansion. All this lawlessness and strife took a heavy toll of lives and created a state of constant uncertainty and unrest.

Notwithstanding these conditions, Formosa steadily developed in commercial importance. The production of sugar, begun at an early date, became profitable and, together with rice, provided a mounting surplus for export to the mainland. The population increased rapidly, until the entire western coastal area became thickly settled.

Decades Preceding Cession to Japan

The first recorded attempt on the part of Westerners, after the Dutch, to open commercial relations with Formosa came with the visit of a British vessel, the *Jamesina* in 1824, but no regular trade was established on that occasion. In 1842, two British vessels, the *Nerbudda* and the *Ann,* were wrecked off the coast of Formosa, and their crews were massacred by order of Chinese officials. Diplomatic protests were made, and the Chinese government degraded and banished the officials responsible. There were also numerous other wrecks of foreign vessels, and there were outrages by the aborigines against their survivors. American vessels, which at that time frequented Far Eastern waters in considerable numbers, were among the principal sufferers. In June 1867 an American naval expedition under the command of Captain Belknap made an ineffectual attempt to take punitive measures against the savages. In the same year, the American consul at Amoy, General le Gendre, undertook a mission to the savages under the military protection of the Chinese and was successful in negotiating arrangements with a chieftain, Tokitok, for civil treatment of shipwrecked foreigners by tribes under his authority.

When the industrial revolution in England created heavy pressure for British trade expansion in the Far East, the strategic position of Formosa with respect to the trade routes in that region attracted the attention of British traders. The acquisition of Hong Kong in 1841, however, satisfied British need of a base for commercial operations. A decade later, when Commodore Perry concluded a treaty with Japan and the American clipper ships were doing a brisk business with Japanese as well as Chinese ports, Americans also began to take an interest in Formosa. The Commodore himself had visited the island in 1854 to investigate reports that American shipwrecked sailors were being held in captivity and to look into the usefulness of coal mines mentioned by earlier American visitors to Keelung. Peter Parker, United States Commissioner to China, and Townsend Harris, first American envoy to Japan, both made recommendations to the Secretary of State advocating that the United States acquire at least a part of the island. Secretary Marcy decisively rejected these suggestions. Subsequently, under the administration of President Bu-

chanan, instructions were given to William B. Reed, who
had been appointed Minister to China, discountenanc-
ing Parker's proposal and emphasizing that the United
States had no territorial ambitions or any other purposes
than those of legitimate commerce.[1] During the Civil
War and for many years thereafter, there was a decline
of American commercial activity in the Far East, and, as
a consequence, Formosa faded out of the sight of most
Americans.

In 1860 two leading British mercantile houses, Jar-
dine Matheson and Company and Dent and Company,
established representatives in Formosa and began to
handle imports of opium and exports of camphor and,
later, of Oolong tea. In the same year, Tamsui and Tainan were opened in pursuance of provisions of the Anglo-
Chinese and the Franco-Chinese treaties. Keelung was
added as a sub-port in 1861 and Takao in 1863. The
first British consular representative arrived at Tamsui
in 1861, and two years later the Chinese government set
up a station of the Imperial Maritime Customs at the
same port. The first American businessmen to establish
themselves locally were Messrs. Field and Hastis, who
formed in 1865 a partnership with a Chinese merchant
to deal in coal and camphor.

For several years the foreign merchants stationed in
Formosa were beset with many difficulties in doing business, arising largely from the hostility of the local official-
dom and populace. The situation in 1870 was so bad
that the British Mission at Peking recommended to the
British Foreign Office that consular representatives be
recalled and that the island be closed to British trade.
Nevertheless, the number of foreign firms grew, and the
volume of foreign trade steadily increased. At that

[1] Tyler Dennett, *Americans in Eastern Asia* (1922), pp. 276-91, 349.

period, the only foreign vessels to call at Formosan ports were small sailing vessels, but in 1871 a fortnightly steamer service to the mainland of China was inaugurated.

In 1871 a Ryukyu vessel was wrecked on the south coast of Formosa, and 54 members of its crew were murdered by Botan tribesmen. Survivors reported this to the home port authorities, who appealed to Tokyo, and the Japanese government made representations at Peking. The Chinese government replied that it could not assume responsibility, because the outrage had been committed outside the territory occupied by the Chinese. The Japanese government decided to act directly. General le Gendre, formerly American Consul at Amoy, was employed as advisor, and an expedition was prepared under the command of General Saigo. The expedition sailed to Formosa in April 1874, and after landing in south Formosa, it did some inconclusive fighting with the savages. Before matters could be brought to a conclusion, however, the Chinese government reversed its position and asserted that the territory of the Formosan savages was within its jurisdiction. The affair then became the subject of diplomatic negotiations between the Chinese and the Japanese governments. The outcome was an agreement under which the Chinese government paid 100,000 taels for the relief of the families of the Ryukyuans who had been murdered and 400,000 taels to the Japanese government for the roads and buildings that the Japanese expeditionary force had constructed. China also undertook to make effective its authority over the savage territory and to protect navigators against injury by the inhabitants. Since that time there have been no further attacks on Westerners by the Formosan aborigines.

In 1884, toward the close of the Franco-Chinese war,
in which Formosa had not been involved, the French
launched an expedition to seize and hold the island as a
guarantee for the payment of an indemnity that France
had exacted from China. A French fleet appeared at
Keelung in August and demanded the surrender of the
forts that guarded the harbor. When the demand was
disregarded by the Chinese, the French took the city by
force. Progress beyond that point was slow and inconclusive. In the course of the subsequent campaign, the
French bombarded Tamsui, blockaded the coast, and
seized the Pescadores. On the main island, however, Chinese resistance was unexpectedly stiff, and the French
never succeeded in gaining control over the island or in
penetrating far into the interior. Although the French
forces on the spot fought bravely and skillfully, the
home authorities had greatly underestimated the needs
of the campaign, and the forces and the commissariat
provided were inadequate to bring about decisive results.
On June 9 a Franco-Chinese treaty was signed which
provided for French evacuation from Formosa and the
Pescadores.

After the retirement of the French, the Imperial Chinese Government, awakened to the strategic importance
of Formosa, decided that it was necessary to introduce
administrative reforms on the island and to emphasize
its economic development. The island was detached from
Fukien and was made a province. The capital was transferred from Taiwan (which was then renamed Tainan)
to Taipei.

The defenses of the island were strengthened. Extensive civic improvements were undertaken at Taipei. The
telegraph line, begun in 1877, was extended from Tainan to Taipei, and a cable was laid between Formosa

and the mainland. In 1891 a narrow-gauge railway was completed between Taipei and Keelung. The line was projected and surveyed to extend through the length of the island to Takao, but from Taipei southward only some 40 miles, to Hsinchu, were completed prior to the Japanese occupation. The original plan for an integrated transportation system contemplated developing a modern port at Keelung, but that feature of the plan was not carried out by the Chinese, and Keelung languished. For a period after the French withdrawal, warfare with the aborigines, largely provoked by Chinese oppression and duplicity in dealing with them was especially severe. Nevertheless, on the whole, the development of Formosa made favorable progress, so much so that the Chinese came to think of the island as a model province. In 1895, however, as a result of the defeat of China in the war with Japan (1894-95), dominion over Formosa passed from China to Japan.

CHAPTER 3.

Formosa Under Japanese Rule

O N MARCH 26, 1895, in the course of the Sino-Japanese war, the Japanese captured the Pescadores
after a brief and ineffectual resistance by the Chinese.
On April 1 a three weeks' armistice was agreed to, in
which, at the instance of the Japanese, Formosa was not
included, and peace negotiations were entered into at
Shimonoseki. Three days before the expiry of the armistice, a peace treaty was signed, and on May 8 this treaty
was ratified by both governments. The treaty provided
for the cession to Japan of Formosa and of the Pescadores, though the Chinese diplomats tried in vain to
soften Japanese insistence on these provisions.

Pacification of the Island

Local Chinese officials and other leaders in Formosa
were not reconciled to the action of the Imperial Chinese Government, and they sent a deputation to Peking
to present a memorial opposing the cession. Overtly at
least, the deputation received no satisfaction, but there
are indications that the secret encouragement and support that it received from officials on the mainland were
in part responsible for the memorial sent on May 23 to
the Emperor at Peking by the Formosan literati, reading
as follows: "The literati and people of Formosa are de-

termined to resist subjection to Japan. Hence they have declared themselves an independent Island Republic, at the same time recognizing the suzerainty of the sacred Tsing Dynasty."[1]

In the meantime, mounting public tension in Formosa had resulted in serious disturbances. This prompted the British to send a warship to protect their nationals. The Germans took similar action, though their interests in the island were negligible. By the time that Japanese transports had arrived at Keelung on May 29 to take possession of the island, a force of 50,000 Formosans had been armed and equipped to dispute the Japanese occupation. The Japanese initially landed a force of 12,000 men and in three days silenced the Keelung forts and cleared the Chinese barracks. While this was going on, the formal ceremonies for the transfer of Formosa between the Chinese and the Japanese plenipotentiaries took place on June 2 on board a Japanese warship near Keelung. In commenting on this event, Yosaburo Takekoshi, a Japanese official has written: ". . . thus the island, which China had torn from Koxinga's descendants by intrigue, bribery and brute force, passed again into the hands of the Japanese, in whose veins flows the same blood as filled those of Koxinga."[2] This florid and misleading statement is characteristic of the effusions of apologists for Japanese imperialism, who were especially conspicuous in the decade following the Russo-Japanese War (1904-05).

Concurrently, there had been a complete breakdown of order and discipline among the Chinese troops in

[1] J. W. Davidson, *The Island of Formosa, Past and Present* (1903), p. 273.
[2] Yosaburo Takekoshi, *Japanese Rule in Formosa* (London, 1907), p. 86.

Taipei. The president of the short-lived Formosan republic, fearing for his life, took flight, and the capital city, its defenses utterly demoralized, was taken in the course of 24 hours by a single Japanese regiment. The Japanese started southward on June 11, and captured Hsinchu (Shinchiku) on the 22nd, but after that the Formosans rallied and began to harry the Japanese seriously by adopting guerrilla tactics.

In the south, General Liu Yung-fu, who had commanded the Chinese forces in the war with France, undertook to reorganize the defense forces. Liu was later "elected" president of a newly formed republic in south Formosa. This republic was also short-lived, and when General Nogi entered the city of Tainan, on October 10, organized resistance came to an end. Even though organized resistance was ended, the Japanese had their hands full for several years in putting down what they described as "banditry" but which in part at least was a movement inspired by the refusal of the Chinese to accept Japanese rule. The most serious difficulty that the Japanese encountered in suppressing disorder stemmed from their inability to enlist the co-operation of the otherwise law-abiding Chinese inhabitants in running the "bandits" down. The peaceful villagers doubtless were influenced by fear of retribution, but they also admired the do-or-die spirit of the outlaws, and they had no love for the Japanese. In some cases, the Japanese soldiery would attack a whole village in the belief that it harbored outlaws, and the survivors and the families of the victims could thenceforth be counted on to cherish a bitter hatred for the conquerors. The "bandits" also had the advantage of knowing the country and of being able to retreat to the jungles and mountains, where the Japanese found it hard to follow them.

Although the Japanese instituted a civil administration in April 1896, no substantial degree of order was established until 1902. Thereafter, the recurrences of "banditry" and uprisings were sporadic rather than chronic. Between 1907 and 1928 there were four armed revolts by Formosan Chinese, all of which were ruthlessly suppressed by the Japanese; and there also was intermittent warfare between the Japanese and the aborigines.

Political and Administrative Patterns

When Japan assumed control of Formosa, it was very conscious of its new position as a colonial power. The Japanese were eager to make their venture a success, not only for profit but to satisfy their pride of possession and to gain repute among the powers. They wanted to be able to point to their colony as evidence that Japan could equal the achievements of other colonizing countries and should be regarded as a great and enlightened power. One manifestation of Japanese nationalism was their welcoming to the blessings of Imperial rule of some millions of new subjects, who would, they assumed, be duly appreciative of this privilege. Although a rescript was issued by the Emperor Meiji calling for the treatment of the Formosans as brothers, the Japanese people, insular in their outlook and unable to enter into imaginative sympathy with other peoples, were ill qualified to carry out the Emperor's injunction. The Japanese administrators, both military and civilian, were gifted with a sense of mechanical order, but lacked the breadth and the vision to fit them for the task of empire building. The military, in addition, were not only arrogant but also were thoroughly imbued with the idea of making the island a base for further Japanese expansion. This mixed motivation is clearly apparent in the character and performance of the Japanese administration of the island.

The Government-General of Formosa was set up as an integral part of the Imperial Japanese Government and operated under the supervision of the Ministry of Home Affairs. In 1929 the Ministry of Overseas Affairs took over this function. The Governor General was regularly an official of the highest rank.[3] The first six appointees successively were generals; the next ten, from October 1919 until September 1926, civilians; after 1936, the appointees were admirals. It is a significant commentary on Japanese political life that it was during the period of civilian governors general that political scandals were most frequent on the islands.

The Governor General wielded wide and, to a large extent, autonomous and autocratic power. He nominated persons for appointment to important positions, and he exercised the appointive power for other positions in the civil administration and for one half the membership of the provincial assemblies. He could cancel or suspend orders of the provincial governors, veto measures of the provincial assemblies, and dissolve the assemblies. If he was an officer in one of the armed services, he was empowered to command the armed forces stationed in the island. He was assisted by a Director General of Civil Administration, an Advisory Council, and an Office of Imperial Affairs.

The Director General of Civil Administration super-

[3] This is the Shinnin grade, that is, an official who receives his appointment in a personal audience with the Emperor. Among officials of this grade are cabinet ministers, ambassadors, full generals and admirals. A governor of a prefecture in Japan is of the next lower grade.

vised the Governor General's Secretariat, the various
administrative bureaus of the government, and the Central Research Institute. The Secretariat was composed
of functionally grouped sections, the numbers and
groupings of which varied from time to time. The Director General also had immediate supervision over the
agencies of local government, for which purpose Formosa was divided into five provinces and three districts.
The Advisory Council comprised both high ranking
officials and prominent civilians, among whom were included Formosans as well as Japanese. The Formosan
members were persons who had closely identified themselves with Japanese interests or whose standing among
their fellow islanders was such that it was politic to
attempt in this way to align them with the administration. The Advisory Council served largely the purpose
of window dressing. The Office of Imperial Affairs had
as its function the co-ordination of military and civil
affairs.

The administration of Formosa was highly central-
ized. Local government was essentially authoritarian
and was in the nature of a field service of the central
administration, with functions that were chiefly fiscal.
The provincial governors, who were appointed rather
than elected, were assisted by provincial assemblies and
provincial councils. The provincial assemblies had vari-
ously from 20 to 40 members, as determined by the
Governor General; one half of them were appointed by
the Governor General and one half elected by the city,
town, or village assemblies. Their functions were purely
advisory. Each provincial council was composed of a
governor, a vice-governor, and six members elected by
and from the provincial assembly. The provincial council acted when the provincial assembly was not in ses-

sion. Since the governor, an appointed official, could veto the measures of a provincial assembly, since one half the members of the assembly were appointees of the Governor General, and since the other half were elected by subordinate units of local government, one half of whose members were appointed by the governor, it would seem that the central administration had made ample provision for ensuring the maintenance of tight control over local government.

This system of local "self-government" was put into force in 1935. In all the provincial and district assemblies, and in all except one of the municipal assemblies, the Japanese members far outnumbered the Formosan members. Only in one municipal assembly and in the village assemblies were there aggregate Formosan majorities. The franchise was limited to male subjects 25 years of age or older who paid local taxes of Yen 5 or more annually. This latter qualification greatly limited the number of eligible Formosans and gave the Japanese a representation greatly disproportionate to their numerical strength. The system aroused criticism in Formosa on this score and was a further source of friction between the Japanese and the Formosans.

Formosa, notorious under the Imperial Chinese regime for its turbulence and lawlessness, was in less than a decade brought by the Japanese into a tolerable degree of order, though the antipathy of the native population to their alien rulers persisted. For administrative control of the population, the conquerors relied upon an elaborate police system. This system comprised a civilian police force, numbering over 12,000 in 1940, supplemented by a special police force of over 5,000 functioning in the areas occupied by the aborigines, and by a military police force numbering some 6,000. This force was backed by a military garrison, which numbered 12,000 before it was increased during the Sino-Japanese conflict of 1937. For the purpose of facilitating the task of the police in controlling the populace, there was brought into play an adaptation and a refinement of the Chinese *paochia* system of group responsibility for the acts of the individual.[4] A *paochia* is a group of approximately 100 households. The head of the group was chosen from among its senior members, but the choice was subject to approval by the county officials and the police. This system worked well in a society where reverence for the head of a patriarchal family has traditionally been the basis of social morality and order, and where property has generally been held by members of a family in common or under common control. In 1940 there were in Formosa nearly 6,000 of these *paochia,* (that is, one per 1,000 of the population). Membership in a *paochia* was not required of Japanese or foreign residents.

The police were charged not only with the preservation of the peace but also with exercise of censorship, supervision of public assembly, regulation of public health, and control of traffic. They exercised a wide and in many respects arbitrary authority over community life. The police relied heavily on the pressures that could be exerted through the *paochia,* on an elaborate system of espionage, and on brutality to keep the Formosans in order. Nor were Japanese civilians and Occidentals entirely immune from overbearing attentions by the police.

The Formosan Chinese were, nevertheless, not politi-

---

[4] In feudal Japan under the Tokugawa Shogunate, a similar technique of social control had been enforced through a system known as *gonin gumi.*

cally inarticulate. As early as 1918, Formosan students in Tokyo organized the Domeikai (league), which was permitted until 1933 to publish a daily organ, the *Taiwan Shimminpo (Formosa Citizen's Report)*. In 1921 the Taiwan Bunka Kyokai (Formosa Cultural Association) was established, and it became a center of a nationalist movement strongly represented in the agricultural co-operatives. This group presented successive petitions to the Japanese Diet asking for representative government for Formosa. The only result was that in 1924 many Formosans were arrested in connection with the petitions, and the leader of the movement for representative government was sentenced to four months imprisonment. Marxist movements also cropped up, but these were soon suppressed. After 1928, when the short-lived political ascendancy of the middle-of-the-road element in Japan ended, there began in Formosa a new era of suppression, which had as its aim the complete elimination of native intellectual leadership. In 1931 the government dissolved the Minseito (Democratic Party) and imprisoned its leaders. The party, whose 800 members were professional and business men, had made an issue of the profiteering of the Japanese government in the operation of the Opium Monopoly.

The outbreak of hostilities between Japan and China in 1937 aggravated the political unrest in Formosa, and the police increased their vigilance in searching for manifestations of sedition. On February 18, 1938, when planes from China bombed airfields near the Formosan capital, all public buildings and strategic crossings were barricaded by sandbags, and machine guns were directed at the Chinese population. So great was the Japanese fear of revolt that the air alarm warning was not sounded until the barricades were up, 3 hours after the raid was ended.

The Japanese occupation had been followed by a heavy Japanese immigration, which was encouraged by the government and by government-supported development companies. Various attempts were made to establish Japanese agricultural settlements in the belief that this would contribute to the success of the assimilation and control program. The program failed to achieve the success hoped for. The Japanese farmers found it difficult to acclimatize themselves and to compete successfully with the Chinese, whose standards of living were much lower. After the first few years there were hardly any Japanese living on the land. The Japanese population thereafter was largely engaged in occupations where they did not enter into competition with the local Chinese: government employees, executive and technical personnel of Japanese business concerns, professional men, hotel keepers and retailers catering to Japanese trade, and persons in personal service to Japanese employers.

Japanese policies with respect to the aborigines differed in many essentials from those directed to the general population. The Japanese inherited in Formosa a legacy of several centuries of misrule, injustice, and inhumanity which had characterized Chinese relations with the aborigines and had produced among the latter a profound distrust and hatred of the Chinese. The state of constant warfare that had resulted was an obstacle to the Japanese objective of developing the economic resources of the entire island, since the aborigines proved as determined to oppose Japanese encroachment upon their domains as they had been to oppose the Chinese.

If the Japanese in the earlier years of their occupation
had adopted a uniform policy of fair dealing and had
exercised patience and tact with the tribesmen, they
might have gained as staunch allies a race possessing
many fine qualities—courage, intelligence, endurance,
and, by primitive standards, high moral character. As it
was, the Japanese were in a hurry to get on with the task
of pacifying the whole island. They deployed troops into
the mountains and jungles, and the jungle-wise tribesmen took a heavy toll. The Japanese in turn became all
the more set on their objectives, but proceeded more
warily and systematically.[5]

The last great uprising of the aborigines took place
at Musha in 1930. This uprising was ruthlessly suppressed by the authorities, and a great many defenseless
and probably innocent tribesmen were killed. This
action caused so much criticism in Japan that it forced
the recall of the Governor General. Eventually, a substantial degree of pacification was achieved, though
never to a point where the territory could be opened to
general settlement or to a normal, peaceful life.

Where they were able to do so, the Japanese disarmed
the tribesmen, who, deprived of means for hunting, were
forced to till the soil for a livelihood. This brought them
down from the mountain heights to the valleys, where
the Japanese could more easily control them. The tribes-

[5] In the course of their campaigns the Japanese destroyed many
villages, some by ground attacks and others by bombing from the air
or, along the east coast, by naval bombardment. Guard lines were extended, which were made by cutting wide lanes along the mountain
tops surrounding the areas inhabited by the tribesmen. At suitable in-
tervals, guard houses were erected, protected by barricades and en-
trenchments, and here soldiers were posted where they could have a
clear vision of the approach of tribesmen. In many places, wire fences
and entanglements, often charged with electricity, were constructed.

men were encouraged to cultivate patches of rice and of other crops, and to raise hogs, buffalos, cattle, goats, and poultry. Tribesmen were also employed by Japanese in outdoor labor, and the women made handwoven baskets and cloth for sale. With little idea of money values, they lent themselves easily to exploitation by the Japanese. Some 200 elementary schools were established which provided a four-year course in the Japanese language and some vocational training.

The Japanese authorities progressively adopted a policy of "Japanization" of the Formosan Chinese. The program became intensified after the outbreak of hostilities with China in 1937. Various methods were adopted to encourage the use of the Japanese language and to discourage the use of Chinese dialects. In the schools, instruction was carried on in the Japanese language only. The police made a record of Formosans conversant with the Japanese language, and persons who were thus recorded found that this enrollment was helpful in applying for licenses of one kind or another and in getting petitions heard. All government and banking business had to be done in Japanese, with the consequence that Formosans not familiar with that language had to talk through interpreters even when conversing with Chinese-speaking clerks.

After 1937 no newspapers were permitted to be published in Chinese or even to carry a Chinese language column. After 1942 when Japan began to foresee the possible eventuality of having to retreat to an "inner zone," Japanese policy underwent modification. The need for gaining the good-will of the Formosans in order to have their co-operation in defending the island began to be recognized, and consequently there was a

relaxation of the compulsory features of the "Japanization" program. The Formosans were even encouraged
to pursue studies in the standard Chinese language.

Social Policies and Measures

As soon as a substantial degree of peace had been established, one of the first of the important tasks to which
the Japanese addressed themselves was that of regulariz-
ing the system of land rights. The Chinese settlers in
Formosa had introduced the system of land tenure
prevalent in the districts from which they came. Those
who had wrested land from the aborigines had achieved
a position comparable to that of feudal lords. They
levied taxes on the persons or groups to whom they
parceled out the land for cultivation. Fortunately for
the tenants, the Fukienese land system recognized a
joint right of landlords and of tenants in the land; no
landlord could arbitrarily evict a tenant or raise his rent.

As time went on, the vigor of the landlord class became sapped by easy living. The tenants had improved
their economic condition, many in turn subletting their
holdings. Eventually, very few persons enjoyed a clear
title to any particular plot of ground, nearly all lands
being owned jointly. The landlord could collect rents
but could not sell the land, while the tenant could sub-
let or could sell his joint interest. These circumstances,
together with the general lack of uniformity in the system of land tenure and the fact that the Chinese administration had made in the course of 200 years no
remeasurements of the land, had created a situation of
almost hopeless confusion.

The Japanese authorities realized that the land system
and the land tax laws are the very foundation of the

social order of an agricultural community and are an important source of public revenue. The policy that they instituted in 1898 was based in part on the precedent afforded by the conversion in 1874 of the feudal holdings in Japan. Land owners were required to report their holdings, and on the basis of the returns a survey was made. The survey, which was completed in 1905, showed a total area of taxable farm land of 1.5 million acres, as compared with 890,000 acres on which taxes were being paid before the survey. When the survey was completed, the government invalidated the land rights of the primary landlords and reimbursed the dispossessed property owner with bonds, just as the feudal lords in Japan had been reimbursed when they surrendered their fiefs.

A valuable contribution made by the Japanese to the improvement of the condition of the farmers was the development, as early as 1907, of farmers' associations. Although the initiative for this development came from the Formosans, whose objectives were to assure their rights in the land and to reduce rents, the Japanese were quick to harness the associations to their own purposes of expanding agricultural production. They applied their characteristic techniques of regimentation to make the associations an effective instrument in carrying out their purposes. Detailed procedures were prescribed for organization and operation and for compulsory recruitment of members. Strict Japanese supervision and control were ensured by making the Governor General the executive head of the federated associations for the whole island and by appointing the principal local officials as ex-officio heads at the prefectural and town or village levels. A corps of Japanese specialists in agriculture was assigned to direct the agricultural improvement work.

The associations were of two kinds, those having as their purpose the financing of agricultural operations and those for educational extension services. The Japanese recognized the need of facilitating the furthering of these purposes and therefore gave the associations substantial subsidies. There was thus created an organization so soundly conceived and developed that it not only has survived the collapse of Japanese rule but will probably remain as the pillar of agricultural co-operative activity in the future. Furthermore, the organization has developed in Formosa a farm population that is more receptive to the application of scientific methods to agriculture than any similar class elsewhere in Asia, except in Japan.

The educational policy adopted for Formosa had as its major purpose the inculcation in the people of a loyalty to the Japanese government. Instruction was in the Japanese language, Chinese being taught only as an advanced technical study. The Formosan Chinese could study their own written language only at home in small groups and after school hours, but they had little incentive to do this because there was not even so much as a weekly newspaper printed in Chinese. In 1939 there were in elementary schools about half a million Formosan Chinese, or about one half of those in the 7-13 age group; in secondary schools, 9,000; in normal schools, 384; and in the university, 90. In contrast 99.4 per cent of the Japanese children were in school; and, although only 5.7 per cent of the population was Japanese, the Japanese students in the higher institutions greatly outnumbered the Chinese Formosans. The fact that many well-to-do Japanese sent their children back to the homeland for their education makes these figures even more striking. The Japanese asserted that there was no discrimination in admission to secondary schools and universities but that the Chinese failed to meet the language requirements. Separate elementary schools were maintained for Japanese children, and Formosan Chinese could be admitted to those schools only by permission of the governor.

In the university, only in the Faculty of Medicine did the number of Chinese students approach that of the Japanese, since the practice of medicine offered the only promising professional career for the Chinese Formosans, other professions being monopolized almost wholly by the Japanese.

The public health service under the Japanese regime was administered by the police, assisted by a branch of the Central Research Institute. The service did well in combating malaria and epidemics, such as small pox and cholera, and it established a standard in general public health administration that was high for the Far East. There were 12 general government hospitals in addition to smaller institutions for chronic ailments and mental cases. The police departments of each of the provincial governments had sanitation bureaus, and the activities of these bureaus, including quarantine measures at the ports, were carried on throughout their respective jurisdictions. In these activities the police had the collaboration of qualified physicians, veterinarians, laboratory technicians, and sanitary inspectors. In 1940 there were in Formosa 298 public and private hospitals, 2,401 physicians, 446 dentists, 349 medical assistants, and 2,026 midwives.

Economic Development

When the Japanese acquired Formosa they were confronted with the problem of providing an income for

an administration that required an annual outlay of
nearly Yen 10 million ($5 million), whereas the esti-
mated tax receipts were only Yen 2.7 million. There
was some dismay in Japan at having acquired a colony
which some thought would prove to be a "white ele-
phant," but this feeling was outweighed by elation at
Japan's having achieved the status of a colonial power.
Consequently, the Diet made little difficulty about ap-
proving subsidies to meet the budgetary deficit. For the
year 1896 the subsidy amounted to nearly Yen 7 million,
but thereafter it was diminished steadily from year to
year until in 1904 it stood at one tenth of the figure for
1896. Although expenditures had doubled during the
same period, the revenues had increased even more
rapidly.[6]

After 1904 Formosa became entirely self-supporting.
In the fiscal year 1943-44, the last year for which budget
figures for the Japanese regime are available, the budget
balanced at Yen 446 million.[7] On the revenue side, net
"receipts from government undertakings and property"
(railways, state forests, and monopolies of camphor, salt,
opium, tobacco, and liquor) were Yen 90 million. Taxes
brought in Yen 121 million. A surplus from the previous
year (underestimating revenues was a normal Japanese
fiscal practice) came to Yen 38 million. The tax burden
thus amounted to Yen 20 (somewhat less than $5 at the
rate prevailing in July 1941) per capita. On the expenditure side, normal operating expenses were greatly exceeded by "non-recurring" items, such as military expenses, encouragement of commerce and industries,

[6] Takekoshi, *Japanese Rule in Formosa*, pp. 133-34.
[7] The United States dollar value of this amount cannot be determined,
as there had been no trade between Japan and the United States since
July 1941, and consequently no exchange rate.

subsidies, and capital expenditures for public enterprises.

The Japanese addressed themselves early in the occupation to the objective of developing the economic
potential of Formosa as a contribution to national
power. This called for an emphasis on programs that
would not only make the most of strategic potentialities
but would also concentrate the control of production
and distribution so as to facilitate mobilization of economic resources.

If economic forces had been allowed to take their
natural course, the authorities would probably not have
diverted, as they did, to sugar growing large areas that
were better adapted to rice production. But rice production did not lend itself as readily as did sugar production
to the manipulation that would provide the maximum
returns to Japan and to native Japanese subjects. The
Formosan farmer's rice crop was something that he could
himself consume or could market without further
processing; his cane crop was salable only to a sugar
mill, and there the farmer had to accept the price that
a few large Japanese sugar operators were willing to
pay. To encourage sugar growing, the Japanese, in addition to giving tariff protection, resorted to various pressures on the Formosan farmers. The shareholders of the
Japanese-owned sugar companies grew rich. This, however, was only partly at the expense of the Formosan
farmers; because of the highly protected market that
Formosa enjoyed in Japan, the Japanese consumers also
contributed to the enrichment of the shareholders.
There was a surplus production over and above what
Japan could take, and this was exported largely to China
and was dumped there usually at a loss since it had to
compete with world prices.

The desire to facilitate regulation by the government of the distribution of the income of productive enterprise undoubtedly influenced the decision of the Japanese authorities to institute government monopolies. Moreover, through monopolies they could collect relatively painlessly an indirect tax, represented by the differences between the selling prices of monopoly products —camphor, opium, salt, tobacco, and liquor—and the prices that would have prevailed in a competitive market.

While the evidence available does not wholly substantiate Japanese assertions that restriction of the opium traffic and reduction of the number of addicts to opium smoking—rather than profits—were the governing considerations in the monopolizing of the opium traffic, the authorities did nevertheless effectively prevent addiction from spreading among the Formosan working class and among the Japanese residents. Each of the two licensed cultivators of coca leaves—the Hoshi Drug Company and the Taiwan Drug Company—was permitted to export from Formosa not more than 50 pounds of cocaine products a month. Hoshi's exports were in the form of dried coca leaves shipped to its factory at Osaka; whereas the Taiwan Drug Company had its factory in Formosa. It is said that under Japanese rule Formosa became one of the principal world sources of cocaine and its derivatives, and thus an important factor in the illicit narcotics traffic conducted by Japanese agents in China.

Under Japanese rule, agriculture continued to be the mainstay of the Formosan economy. Productivity was greatly expanded through bringing new lands under cultivation and through the introduction of scientific methods. At the end of 1941 there were 3 million people, or one half the entire population, engaged in farm-

ing; about one third were owner cultivators, another
third tenant cultivators, and the final third part tenant
part owner cultivators. The total area under cultivation
increased from 864,000 acres in 1899 to 2,111,000 acres
in 1941. The most important crop was rice. Two crops of
rice annually yielded approximately 42 million bushels,
or about 27 bushels per acre. The Japanese had introduced their own type of rice (similar to that grown in
California), and more than half the Formosan crop was
exported to Japan.

Second in importance among the agricultural products of Formosa was sugar. Under Chinese rule, sugar
milling had been carried on in primitive plants in which
animal power was used for pressing. The methods used
were wasteful, and the product was inferior. The first
modern-type mills were put into operation by the
Taiwan Seito, founded in 1901, in which the Japanese
Imperial Household was an important investor. By 1941
the sugar manufacturing industry was almost entirely
in the hands of six Japanese companies, with an aggregate capital of Yen 217 million ($52 million), operating
49 modern mills; the total sugar production, crude and
refined, was somewhat over a million metric tons.

During the Japanese occupation the prosperity of the
tea trade declined considerably. This was due in part
at least to the Japanese discouragement of British and
American export tea buyers established in Formosa. The
Japanese were prompted by a desire to get the trade into
their own hands. The tea trade, however, required a
specialized knowledge of consumers' markets and tastes,
and in this the Japanese were at a disadvantage as compared with British and American tea buyers and therefore in foreign marketing.

Other principal agricultural crops were sweet potatoes

(367,000 acres in 1941), peanuts (28,000 acres), beans (25,000 acres), and sesamum (16,000 acres). From the standpoint of exports, however, the banana crop was more important than any other agricultural crop except rice and sugar. Under Japanese rule the growing and canning of pineapples was developed into a flourishing industry, ranking next, it is said, only after the pineapple industries of Hawaii and of Malaya. Other important fruits cultivated were the orange, the pomelo (which is closely related to the grapefruit), and the lungan (which is related to the Chinese lychee and has a vinous flavor). Livestock consisted principally of buffalos (266,000), hogs (1.2 millions), and poultry (8 millions).

Eighty-nine per cent of the total forest area of nearly 6 million acres was government-owned. Under Chinese rule, there had been a reckless cutting of forests, but the Japanese established in 1915 a Forestry Bureau which adopted a policy of forest protection and a program of reforestation. Sales from lumber in government forests in 1940 were valued at approximately $1.8 million.

Of chief interest among the forest resources of Formosa is the camphor tree. Straight-trunked and well-formed, this tree attains an enormous size. Some trees have been observed with a circumference of 40 feet, but most of the trees felled range around 12 feet, and one of these will yield some 6,000 pounds of crystals.[8]

[8] These crystals are produced by distillation in the forests where the wood abounds. Chips from the felled trees are placed in kilns and distilled. Fifty pounds of chips will yield on the average one pound of camphor crystals and about four ounces of camphor oil, the amounts varying according to the season, the efficiency of the kiln, and the skill of the operator. Under the Japanese, the crude camphor thus obtained was refined at the Camphor Monopoly plant at Taipei.

The trees large enough for profitable cutting occur generally interspersed here and there in stands of different species of trees. The

Fisheries, with a catch in 1940 valued at about $9.2 million, and mining, with an output in 1937 valued at $8.6 million, complete the list of extractive industries. The greater part of the mineral output was coal and gold (including gold and gold-copper ores). Total coal reserves were estimated by the Japanese at 400 million metric tons. The average annual output between 1940 and 1944 was about 2.4 million tons. Very little of the coal is of a grade suitable for coking.

The total value of manufactures in private industry in 1940 was about $137 million, of which two thirds was from sugar. Other processed products that exceed $1 million in value were tea, canned pineapple, machinery and tools, mixed fertilizers, printed matter, woodwork, paper, confectionery, macaroni, hemp cloth, and cement. Production of refined camphor by the government monopoly in 1935, a record year, amounted to 700 metric tons. In the later years of their rule the Japanese introduced the manufacture of aluminum, using as a raw material bauxite imported from the Netherlands East Indies.

Formosa is adapted to cheap production of hydroelectric power. As early as 1931 the Japanese began to develop, with an American loan amounting to $22.8 mil-

---

heaviest growths of such trees have always been along the fringes of the central mountain area. This was a primary cause of the steady encroachment of the Chinese upon the aborigines. The Chinese customarily resorted to sharp dealing and trickery as well as force in making their advances. The aborigines retaliated as opportunity offered by ambushing the camphor gatherers, and the Chinese countered with attacks upon and destruction of the tribesmen's villages. Conflicts between Chinese settlers and Chinese government authorities also took a toll. In the 1720's the latter decapitated some 200 persons for illicit felling of camphor trees, a practice that had been prohibited by the government. This precipitated a revolt—which was put down only after much bloodshed. In the course of Formosa's history, the exploitation of camphor was thus attended by the loss of thousands of lives.

lion, an extensive hydroelectric plant at Lake Candidius (Jitsugetsutan), a project that was completed in 1934. The potential hydroelectric capacity of all Formosan rivers has been estimated at 2.5 million kilowatt hours. In the year of peak production, 1943, there were generated 1.2 million kilowatt hours.

Between 1897 and 1939 the Yen value of Formosa's foreign trade increased 32 fold.[9] In the latter years, exports amounted to about $142 million and imports to $98 million. Eighty-six per cent of the exports and 87 per cent of the imports were in trade with Japan. The remainder of the trade was largely with the United States and adjacent Asian countries. Actual trade with the United States was, however, substantially larger than the Japanese customs figures would indicate, because of the indirect shipments through Japan which were credited to Japanese trade. Except for the export trade in tea and the import trade in petroleum products, which were handled largely by British and American firms having establishments in Formosa, together with some junk-borne trade conducted by Chinese merchants between the island and adjacent Chinese ports, the foreign trade of Formosa was almost entirely in the hands of Japanese firms. The domestic trade of the island, however, was to a large extent conducted by Formosan Chinese.

The only regular sailings to and from Formosa were by Japanese vessels, which maintained cargo and passenger services chiefly with Kobe, Shanghai, and Hong Kong. Internal transportation was provided by a network of fairly good roads and 890 miles of railway (565 miles of which were government-owned).

[9] Because of the drop in the exchange value of the yen the increase in the dollar value was only 16 fold.

There were no European or American banking establishments in Formosa. Foreign exchange banking facilities were provided almost exclusively by the Bank of Taiwan. This was a semiofficial institution, empowered to issue notes. It had, in addition to its facilities in Formosa, 31 branches and 2 agencies in Japan and foreign countries.

The Bank of Taiwan and the Taiwan Development Company were the principal economic instruments of Japanese adventurings southward that were spearheaded from Formosa. The Taiwan Development Company was established as a semiofficial organ; for its creation the government put up half the initial capital of Yen 30 million. Its declared objectives were: (a) land reclamation; (b) the promotion of agricultural and forestry enterprises to supply strategic materials lacked by Japan; (c) settlement of Japanese immigrant farmers, (d) financing of other colonization enterprises, and (e) management of economic enterprises generally in the southeast Asian area. It controlled, for example, companies that supplied light and water both to Canton and to Amoy in China, and it organized various enterprises in Hainan Island. It had mining interests in Malaya and in Indo-China, and cotton enterprises in Thailand.

Another device which the Japanese developed for expansion directed from Formosa was the organization and training of agents recruited from the Formosan-Chinese population. Formosan Chinese who were subservient to Japanese interests were employed extensively by the Japanese for espionage and other devious activities in the adjacent areas of south China. These Formosans, being Japanese subjects and therefore protected by the extra-territorial rights that Japan enjoyed in China, habitually made the most of their immunity from Chinese jurisdiction. This led to bad blood between the islanders and the mainlanders and contributed ultimately to the difficulties that arose and the rigorousness with which the islanders were treated after the Chinese reoccupied the island in 1945.

Formosa and the Second World War

During the Second World War, Formosa made, according to the *Japan Year Book*,[10] "invaluable contributions toward the southward movement of the Imperial Army and Navy."

With the outbreak of the war, the Governor General proclaimed a National General Mobilization, in which emphasis was placed on "the spiritual unity of all the races in the island." Control measures were instituted to promote increased production and exports, to regulate prices and the distribution of commodities and of the labor supply, and to restrict imports. There was a complete conscription of labor to provide such army labor service as was needed. Except for a small corps of aborigines, known as the Takasago Volunteer Unit, used for scouting and supply work in jungle fighting, the use made of the non-Japanese man power of Formosa as a source of combat strength was negligible. This was ascribable to the fact that the Japanese could not rely on the Chinese to be loyal to their alien rulers in such a service.

In the war preparations of Japan, Formosa was developed as a naval and air base. It played an important part as a staging point for the southward movement of troops, ships, and material. Numerous airfields were constructed, especially in the southwest part of the island,

[10] *Japan Year Book, 1943-44*, p. 921.

and ports and warehouse facilities were improved. It was from Formosa that the initial air attacks on the Philippines were launched, as well as the subsequent invasion of those islands. Formosa provided bases for surface vessels and submarines, and afforded safe anchorage for convoys. In the latter part of the war, when United States naval superiority was established in the western Pacific and American aircraft carriers were brought into action, American planes were able to neutralize Formosa by bombing airfields, destroying the Japanese planes grounded there, and demolishing military installations. After that, Formosa became a liability rather than an asset to Japan. However, since it was not needed by the American forces as a base for the assault on Japan, it was not seized during the hostilities.

Over-All Appraisal of Japanese Rule

In retrospect, Japanese rule on Formosa appears to have had both good points and bad. The primary aims of the rulers were to augment the resources and contribute to the glory of the empire by developing the island for profit and as a base for expansion southward. The Japanese officials and services addressed themselves with unflagging energy to the realization of these objectives. The wealth that they developed was incidentally shared by the islanders, who came to enjoy a standard of living conspicuously higher than that of their brethren on the mainland of China.

The official policy envisaged assimilation, but in the half century of Japanese rule little progress was made in that direction. The Formosans clung to their Chinese dress and mode of life and language. They were looked down upon by the Japanese, few of whom deigned to learn even a smattering of the Chinese language. The two races kept almost entirely apart socially and culturally. Consequently, the Japanese never succeeded in winning the respect, the affection, or the loyalty of their Formosan subjects. .

No opportunity was offered the natives for cultural or political self-expression. For the most part the doors to executive, professional, and technical positions in government and business were closed to them. As a result, when the Japanese relinquished control, there was in the island no substantial body of Formosans with the requisite training and experience to take over political leadership and economic management.

Official corruption and abuse of authority were by no means absent, but many observers have been impressed with the probity and the earnestness of purpose of the majority of the higher Japanese officials with whom they came into contact, and with the simplicity of their mode of life. There is evidence also that the island did not suffer under Japanese rule the degree of oppression that Korea and Manchuria did when they likewise were under Japanese rule. In Formosa, the Japanese provided at least a degree of law and order and protection for property and person that, according to available accounts, had not been known before.

Much of what the Japanese had built on the island, such as factories, dams, and communication and transportation facilities, was destroyed in the course of the war as a result of allied bombing from the air. Japan's principal legacy to the island was the impress that Japanese rule had made on the Formosan people. The severance of the island from China had occurred during the Manchu regime, and the inhabitants of Formosa did not share the experience of China's Republican Revolution of 1912 or of the Nationalist unification of China in the following decades. The Formosans were shielded from the convulsions of political and social change that wracked China. As a consequence, the Formosan leaders were, and are, far behind their mainland brethren in political sophistication. At the same time the Formosans were in some respects more advanced than the mainland Chinese. The Formosans had learned under the Japanese occupation what it was to live under a rule of law, which, though stern, was effectively administered. They also had learned what can be accomplished toward increasing productive power and improving standards of living through large-scale, efficiently conducted, systematic and co-operative effort. In the acquisition of this knowledge they were spared, thanks to their Japanese rulers, much of the blind groping, false starts, and frustrations that the Chinese people on the mainland have experienced.

PART TWO

DEVELOPMENTS SINCE
WORLD WAR II

CHAPTER 4.

Wartime Planning and Early Postwar Events

I N THE Cairo Declaration issued jointly by President Roosevelt, Prime Minister Churchill, and President Chiang Kai-shek on December 1, 1943, it was declared that it was the "purpose" of the "three Great Allies" that "all the territories Japan had stolen from the Chinese, such as Manchuria, Formosa and the Pescadores, shall be returned to the Republic of China." In the Potsdam Proclamation of July 26, 1945, signed by the President of the United States and the Prime Minister of the United Kingdom, and concurred in by the President of China and subsequently adhered to by the Soviet Union, it was agreed that the terms of the Cairo Declaration were to be carried out.

Wartime Planning

The Cairo Declaration was the starting point for planning by the United States Government for the initial postwar treatment of Formosa. A number of questions arose in this connection. The first was: What would be the legal status of the Island between the time of a Japanese surrender and the formalizing of a Japanese cession of it to China under a treaty of peace? That is, would sovereignty continue to rest in Japan during this period, or would it reside with the United Nations? Or, again, if Formosa were handed over to China for administration, would sovereignty also pass at the same time? Entirely apart from the legal principles involved, it was apparent that in practical application a clear-cut ruling in favor of any of these three positions would present difficulties for the United States. In the quandary thus produced, the United States Government made no public pronouncement at all on the subject. Nevertheless, the general thinking after the Japanese surrender was that although, by signing the Instrument of Surrender, Japan had relinquished sovereignty over the Island, and although the Chinese reoccupied Formosa and assumed an *interim* administrative authority, legal transfer of that sovereignty to China would require formalization by a treaty of peace.

It was believed however, that China did not have the shipping tonnage requisite to ferry over to Formosa personnel to receive the Japanese surrender and to assume administrative functions, to say nothing of the military strength that would be needed if armed resistance were encountered. It was therefore obvious that United States assistance would have to be given to enable the Chinese Government to effect a successful reoccupation. It was assumed that such operations as might be needed to occupy Formosa would be under an American theater commander, who, accordingly, would be responsible for the establishment and the conduct of the military administration of civil affairs there. Moreover, it was contemplated that such administration would continue pending the regularization by treaty of the future status of Formosa. The possibility that the period of non-treaty status would be of long duration was not then foreseen. In United States Navy circles especially, there was a strong feeling that the United States should continue to exercise the authority of a military occupant pending the formal assumption by China of sovereignty.

There was some question in Service circles whether the occupation of Formosa, if carried out, should be an Army or a Navy responsibility. Eventually, by common consent, the Navy undertook the task of preparing for such an undertaking. Training of personnel for military government was instituted at Columbia University. There was still lacking, however, guidance with respect to American political objectives. On this point, the Navy and the Army sought the advice of the Department of State.

The detailed recommendations that the Department of State made in the spring of 1944 were based on the considerations and assumptions to which reference has already been made. It was known that the Chinese Government for its part had been making preparations to take over the island. Inasmuch as the population of Formosa was predominantly Chinese, and as the island was eventually to be turned over to China, it was thought that Chinese co-operation in military government would be helpful and would tend, when the time came, to facilitate a smooth turning over to China. Nevertheless, it was considered that, while the participation of Chinese as individuals and in an advisory capacity would be welcomed, the United States should not ask the Chinese Government to take part in this administration. It was proposed that the Chinese Government be informed of the general decisions that the United States Government might take with respect to the establishment of the civil affairs administration, and that the American plans should conform, so far as possible, with China's program for the future of the island.

Decisions on the extent to which Chinese personnel would be taken into the administration would, it was thought, have to depend upon the extent of Chinese military participation in the military operations for occupation of Formosa.

At the time, no action or top-level decision was taken on these recommendations. They were laid aside to await developments in the military situation in the Pacific theater. A plan was formulated for the seizure of Formosa to precede the occupation of the Philippines, but this plan was abandoned as impracticable. Formosa was neutralized, however, by carrier air attack. In the course of the allied advance on Japan after the recovery of the Philippines, Formosa was by-passed in favor of an attack on Okinawa. The capture of Okinawa on June 21, 1945, obviated the need of seizing Formosa for use as a staging area for the contemplated final assault on the Japanese home islands.

It has been asserted that President Roosevelt had by early 1945 made up his mind that China was to be given possession of Formosa as soon as Japan should surrender. If this were the case, the President's view was apparently not then communicated to personnel at planning levels. Nevertheless, coincidentally with the American occupation of Okinawa, there was a marked change in the thinking in Army and Navy circles with regard to an American military occupation of Formosa. A general consensus appears to have been reached by the planners that only if Formosa were taken by United States forces in the course of combat operations would it be necessary to establish a military government there, and that in such event the island should be turned over to the Chinese as soon as this could be arranged without awaiting the formalization by treaty of Chinese sovereignty over the island. It was also envisaged that if an American military government was not established in consequence of combat operations, Formosa would be occupied and administered by the Chinese from the outset.

On August 14, 1945 the Japanese government announced its acceptance of the Potsdam terms as a basis for surrender. In the United States Government there was prepared a draft of General Order No. 1 to be issued by the Japanese Government for implementing the surrender terms. This document provided among other things that the surrender of the Japanese armed forces in Formosa would be taken by Generalissimo Chiang Kai-shek. The question thus became further clarified, and it was then considered that only if the Chinese were unable to establish control or if military necessity should arise would the United States need to concern itself further with the matter. Finally, in September, after the Japanese surrender, when it was determined that Chinese forces were prepared to move with American aid by an amphibious lift into Formosa, consideration of plans for an American military government was dropped.[1]

Chinese Reoccupation

In September 1945 the administration of Formosa was taken over from the Japanese by Chinese forces assisted by numerically small United States teams pursuant

[1] Available documentary material on the foregoing sequence of events is fragmentary. The account given here has been pieced together largely from recollections of the present writer, who was Director of the Office of Far Eastern Affairs in the Department of State during much of the period when these matters were being considered, and who thus can speak from first hand knowledge of some phases of the case, and from the recollections and impressions of Army and Navy officers and officials of the Department of State whom he has consulted in the preparation of this study.

to the Japanese Instrument of Surrender and to General
Order No. 1. The Japanese Instrument of Surrender
did not mention Formosa specifically, but it stipulated
complete acceptance and fulfillment of the terms of the
Potsdam Proclamation, which had confirmed the provisions of the Cairo Declaration.

Although it had been assumed by the United States
Government that China, upon its reoccupation of Formosa, would constitute that island as a province on a
parity with the provinces on the mainland, the Chinese
administration that was inaugurated on October 3,
1945 assumed the character of a military government
under an "Administrator General and Concurrently
Supreme Commander in Taiwan Province." General
Chen Yi, a member of the professedly liberal Political
Science Clique of the Kuomintang, which party at that
time still dictated the policies of the National Government of China, was appointed to this post.

The Formosan Chinese, who had been led to expect
that with their liberation from the Japanese they would
be reunited on terms of equality with their mainland
brethren, welcomed the new administration. They
looked forward to a realization of their aspirations for
self-rule and to taking over the management and enjoy-
ing the profits of the enterprises developed, with assistance from them, by the Japanese. Their expectations
were short-lived, for it soon became apparent that Formosa was to be treated as a conquered territory, and its
population as a subjugated people.

It had already been decided by the National Government that after V-J Day the Government would take over
all Japanese assets in China (including Formosa). Inasmuch as the greater part of the productive enterprise on

the Island was Japanese owned and operated, and, moreover, since the Chinese Government proceeded on the
presumption that most Formosans of any standing under
the Japanese regime had been Japanese collaborationists,
the applying of the policy called for comprehensive ex-
propriation of business undertakings.

Chen Yi and his associates lost no time in beginning
to reorganize the Japanese enterprises into a system of
officially operated monopolies. It is estimated that at
least 90 per cent of all economic enterprises on the island were thus brought under governmental control.[2]
Formosan employees, regardless of their experience and
ability, were replaced by Chinese from the mainland.
Although staffs of technicians and engineers with
modern training were brought in, they were unable to
achieve the results of which they were capable because
they lacked the authority to control the relatives and
friends of the governing clique who swarmed over to the
island and were put in positions of authority. Many of
the enterprises were stripped of all movable capital assets, which were sold or otherwise disposed of to the
mainland. Some of the enterprises did not resume operations at all, and others were forced by incompetent and
reckless management sooner or later to close down or to
curtail operations. The staffs of new employees were
retained, however, as long as there were capital assets or
government subsidies from which salaries could be paid.
Even individual enterprises did not escape the greed
of the new authorities and their henchmen. A licensing
system was introduced that required permits for all business activity of private individuals. This became a means

[2] "Formosa in Transition," *The World Today*, Vol. 4 (May 1948),
p. 213.

for imposing arbitrary exactions that soon reduced the Formosan merchant and professional classes almost to beggary, and private enterprise almost disappeared.

So intent were the mainland "carpet-baggers" upon achieving quick profits that they paid little attention to the pressing need for rehabilitation as a means of restoring the productive capacity of the island. Shortages developed in the supply of rice, which the authorities attributed to illegal hoarding by Formosans, but which the Formosans charged, with substantial evidence, was accounted for by unpublicized shipments of the grain to feed the Nationalist armies on the mainland. The draining away of wealth was quickly reflected in soaring prices. The Bank of Taiwan wholesale price indexes, based on June 1937, showed advances between November 1945 and January 1947 as follows: foodstuffs, 3,323 to 21,058; clothing, 5,741 to 24,483; fuel 963 to 14,091; fertilizers 129 to 37,559, and building materials 949 to 13,612.[3]

There was a breakdown in the quarantine and public health services, with the result that cholera epidemics and bubonic plague, after an absence of almost a generation, reappeared. Educational standards fell, and public morals deteriorated.

Three announcements by the Government, made early in 1946, in particular aroused bitter resentment among the Formosans. These were: (1) a decision that Formosans would not be permitted to have local self-government until December 1949, though the new Chinese constitution was to go into effect on the mainland two years earlier; (2) a plan for the disposal of former Japanese property which Formosans regarded as virtu-

[3] U. S. Department of State, *United States Relations with China* (August 1949), p. 924.

ally excluding those not possessed of great wealth and influence from acquiring such properties; and (3) the promulgation of a series of complicated trading and financial regulations the effect of which, the Formosans believed, would be to establish a monopolistic control of business in the hands of a small group of officials. The adoption of these policies seemed to the Formosans to foreshadow the return of the islanders to the subservient position from which they had suffered under the Japanese occupation and to threaten the destruction of the means by which they had hoped to develop for themselves the resources of the island.[4]

The conduct of the Chinese officials was in part attributable to the fact that they found in Formosa a standard of living, a degree of material progress, and a disposition on the part of the populace to stand up for their property rights (as distinct from political rights) such as were little known on the mainland. These conditions aroused both the cupidity of the officials and a determination to tolerate no resistance to their authority. The Formosans, for their part, who were accustomed to an organized and disciplined society under a rule of law, compared unfavorably the conduct of business and government under the new regime with that which had prevailed under the Japanese.

In these circumstances, it was perhaps natural that the Formosans should be disposed to magnify the responsibility of Chinese officials for the deplorable economic plight of the Island and to overlook the effects of allied bombings and years of disruption of normal life. Under such conditions, the rapid rehabilitation of the island could hardly have been expected even under a more beneficent administration. Consequently, the ex-

[4] The same, pp. 925, 926.

pectations of the Formosans of an early alleviation of their misfortunes might in any case have been doomed to disappointment.

Such was the background of the violent clash which took place in the second year of the Chinese occupation.

Formosan Revolt of 1947 and Its Aftermath

On February 27, 1947 special agents of the Tobacco Monopoly killed a woman who had been hawking tax-not-paid cigarettes. On the following day a large crowd of Formosans made an orderly march to the Tobacco Monopoly headquarters to demand redress. Receiving no satisfaction there, they moved on toward the Governor's office. When they reached an adjacent wide intersection, they were fired upon by the police and at least four of them were killed. This prompted a general attack on the occupation authorities by the Formosans, both in Taipei and elsewhere, and the proclamation by the authorities of martial law. The Formosans organized a "Committee for the Settlement of the February 28th Incident." Chen Yi, who then lacked the necessary military forces to cope with a revolt, adopted a temporizing attitude and accepted in principle a series of demands which included an agreement that he would consider various measures of political and economic reform of which a list was to be drawn up. He entered into an arrangement whereby, in return for an engagement by the Formosans to cease from violence, he would move no troops into the city and would gradually eliminate the bands of roving police patrols.

However, Chen's complete lack of good faith was soon revealed. While a program of reforms was still under consideration, he took advantage on March 8 of the arrival of reinforcements from China, said to have numbered over 50,000, to institute massacres of Formosans at Taipei and elsewhere, in the course of which some 10,000 Formosans were killed. A systematic effort was made to eliminate the principal native leaders. By the end of March the island had been cowed into submission.

The news of these events spread abroad rapidly and was highly prejudicial to the effort of the National Government to show that it was trying to make progress toward democratic reforms. President Chiang Kai-shek despatched General Pai Chung-hsi to the island to investigate and report. Pai commanded general public confidence in China because of his long record for probity, for maintenance of discipline in his entourage, and for his independence of character. Nevertheless, his report, or what was given out as purporting to be his report, stated that the revolt was due to Communist instigation, to the effects on Formosans of Japanese training, and to the machinations of ambitious Formosan politicians.

There is little evidence, however, that communism had spread widely in Formosa. The effect of Japanese training, in this instance, was to make Formosans more disposed than mainland Chinese to stand up for their rights. At the same time, the Formosan leaders had shown a commendably restrained and conciliatory attitude in their dealings with the Chinese authorities, and had taken great pains to emphasize that their effort was directed toward good government, with a view to making Formosa a model province of China.

After order had been substantially restored, the United States Ambassador at Nanking called the attention of President Chiang Kai-shek to the deplorable state of affairs in Formosa. The Ambassador pointed out that the measures which had been instituted there were destroying a source of wealth that was desperately needed at that time. Chiang, who said that he was unaware of conditions as they were reported to him by the Ambassador, requested that a memorandum be prepared for him setting forth in detail conditions as the American officials saw them. Such a memorandum was presented to President Chiang on April 18. It contained a statement of what had occurred on the island in much greater detail than is given above.[5]

Within a month after the Generalissimo had received the Ambassador's memorandum, General Chen Yi was relieved of his post and was succeeded by Wei Tao-ming, who had recently been Chinese Ambassador to the United States.[6] The island was made a province, one of the 35 provinces of China. The chief magistrate was given the title of Chairman of the Provincial Council, in conformity with the practice followed in all the other provinces. The Council that was formed consisted of 14 members, half of whom were islanders, most of them with mainland experience. The great majority of Chen Yi's associates were replaced by new appointees, and among these a goodly proportion were Formosans. The Chairman was given jurisdiction over the armed forces, censorship was officially lifted, and the end of the "pacification" was announced.

During his term in office of a year and a half, Wei

[5] The same, pp. 307-10, 923-38. See also George Kerr, "Formosa's Return to China," *Far Eastern Survey* Oct. 15-Nov. 5, 1947, Vol. 16, pp. 205-08, 224-26. See also, "Formosa in Transition," *World Today,* Vol. 4, May 1948, pp. 209-17.

[6] After his recall Chen Yi was appointed governor of Chekiang Province, but in June 1950 he was removed from that post and was executed on conviction of having planned a year earlier to sell out the province to the communists.

Tao-ming made an honest effort to undo the ill effects of Chen Yi's misgovernment. In a radio address soon after his assumption of office, he expressed himself in favor of free enterprise. The Monopoly Bureau was abolished, a Tobacco and Liquor Bureau was created, the Camphor Company was placed under the Department of Reconstruction, and a Material Supply Adjustment Committee was established to take over the functions of the Taiwan Trading Bureau, which was discontinued. A number of government enterprises, such as the Match Company, were opened to private operation and investment. Mining and industrial concerns, jointly operated by government and private interests, were also turned over to private hands. Unemployment relief measures were undertaken, and the Chairman himself attempted to keep the island free from the inflationary and disruptive forces that were at work on the mainland. Many of his key officials were, however, unresponsive to Wei's efforts. On the whole, although it cannot be said that economic conditions improved forthwith, the situation did not become appreciably worse.

In the course of his mission to China, General Albert Wedemeyer on August 14, 1947, reported to the Secretary of State as follows:

Our experience in Formosa is most enlightening. The administration of the former Governor Chen Yi has alienated the people from the Central Government. Many were forced to feel that conditions under autocratic rule were preferable. The Central Government lost a fine opportunity to indicate to the Chinese people and to the world at large its capability to provide honest and efficient administration. They cannot attribute their failure to the activities of the Communists or dissident elements. The people anticipated sincerely and enthusiastically deliverance from the Japanese yoke. However, Chen Yi and his henchmen ruthlessly, corruptly and avariciously imposed their regime upon a happy and amenable population. The Army conducted themselves as conquerors. Secret Police operated freely to intimidate and to facilitate exploitation by Central Government officials. . . .

The island is extremely productive in coal, rice, sugar, cement, fruits and tea. Both hydro and thermal power are abundant. The Japanese had efficiently electrified even remote areas and also established excellent railroad lines and highways. Eighty per cent of the people can read and write, the exact antithesis of conditions prevailing in the mainland of China. There were indications that Formosans would be receptive toward United States guardianship and United Nations trusteeship. They fear that the Central Government contemplates bleeding their island to support the tottering and corrupt Nanking machine and I think their fears well founded.[7]

By the latter part of 1948 the deterioration that had set in within the ranks and in the affairs of the National Government was producing a spirit of defeatism, and Generalissimo Chiang Kai-shek was giving increasing attention to creating in Formosa, as he had years before done in Szechwan, a last resort stronghold from which Nationalist resistance might be continued. As one preparatory move, Chiang decided to replace Wei Tao-ming as Governor of Formosa with General Ch'en Ch'eng. The shift was made on January 5, 1949. The new Governor lost no time in reasserting martial law. There followed a wave of arrests and executions of persons charged with being Communist sympathizers. Economic conditions became worse, and there was a recession from the gains that had been made during Wei's regime toward establishing confidence among the Formosans.

[7] U. S. Department of State, *United States Relations with China*, p. 309.

CHAPTER 5.

Collapse of National Government on China's Mainland

W HILE the events described in the preceding Chapter were taking place in Formosa, profound changes occurred within the borders of China on the mainland. These changes finally culminated in a complete military victory of the Communist forces and the removal to Formosa in December 1949 of the seat of the National Government. For the second time in the history of China, a government defeated on the mainland took refuge on the "beautiful island."

Before considering the problems that arose when Formosa became the seat of the National Government, it is necessary to review briefly the main features of the developments within China that had led to the collapse and flight of the National Government. These developments had their roots in the long series of internal and external changes that had occurred over several decades of Chinese history.

Basis of China's Internal Strife

Since the beginning of the twentieth century, the internal political situation in China has been characterized by an acceleration of the process of social change that had been set in motion at least a half a century earlier by the necessity of making adjustments to the impact and challenge of the Western World. At times, this process of change took revolutionary forms. An important phase of it was the overthrow of the Manchu Dynasty and the setting up of the Republic in 1911-12.

Some years earlier, Dr. Sun Yat-sen, a native of a south China district which had a long tradition of foreign intercourse, had organized a revolutionary movement. Dr. Sun had received a modern education at Hong Kong and in Hawaii. Many of his early supporters were natives of his own province of Kwangtung, some were Chinese living abroad, and some had been Chinese students in Japan or in the new "modern" schools and colleges in China. Although Dr. Sun was elected President by a group of his followers, he yielded in favor of Yuan Shih-kai, a leading figure in the Imperial bureaucracy. Thus Dr. Sun and his followers were denied for many years the rewards of their work.

They retreated to the South and reorganized the Kuomintang, or National Party. This reorganization, carried out under Russian advice, provided for a single party system of government. The Party, thus revitalized and aided by Russian Communist advisers, who were headed by Michael Borodin, organized an army and instituted at Canton a program based upon Dr. Sun's political and economic theories. In 1924, on the advice of Borodin, many members of the Chinese Communist party, which had been organized in 1921, were admitted by Dr. Sun to the Kuomintang.

Dr. Sun outlined his political doctrines in the "Three Principles of the People," a symposium of his "lectures." His great concern was, not to achieve more freedom for the individual, but to achieve freedom and unity for the nation. Dr. Sun's program called for national reconstruction in three stages: a military stage, to continue until all China should be reunited under the Kuomintang (which between 1924 and 1926 held only the Canton area); a stage of "political tutelage" under the one-party dictatorship of the Kuomintang, to last until the citizens of a majority of the provinces were prepared to exercise political rights; and a final stage of constitutional government.

Sun Yat-sen died in 1925, but his influence thereafter increased. The three principles became sacrosanct among all factions of the party, though they were subjected to wide latitudes of interpretation and application.

In 1926 the newly organized Nationalist army under Chiang Kai-shek started northward. With it went Communist forces. After a succession of easy victories, in the course of which Hankow, Nanking, and Shanghai were taken and the Communist cadres and, later, the Soviet advisers were jettisoned, the Nationalist forces reached Peking in 1928. After the capture of Peking, the Nationalists removed the capital to Nanking and established the "National Government of the Republic of China." With this, the military stage of national reconstruction theoretically came to an end and the period of "political tutelage" began.

In its development after 1923, the Kuomintang was a composite of groups and individuals of all shades of political opinion, brought together by a common desire to terminate the rule of the war lords and unify the country. From the outset, the radical and the conservative elements in the Nationalist movement had been divided, but after the capture of Shanghai and Nanking, a breach developed which culminated in the purging of the Communist elements from the Kuomintang, the execution or killing in battle of large numbers of the Communists and the expulsion of the Russian advisers. However, an armed remnant made good a retreat to the hinterland of Kiangsi Province where it carried on a stubborn resistance against the National Government. In 1934 that group, augmented by new recruits, began a mass march which ultimately took them into Shensi Province in northwestern China. Here they instituted, with the tolerance of the National Government, an independent jurisdiction over a small area around the city of Yenan.

A truce was effected, in outward appearance, in 1937 by the formation of a "united front" against Japanese aggression. Hostilities began again in 1941 when National and Communist forces clashed because the Communist troops moved beyond the military zones assigned to them. Thenceforth the National Government ceased to pay and to supply the Communist forces and attempted, by a military blockade, to isolate them from the rest of China.

The fundamentally conflicting aims of the Kuomintang and the Chinese Communists and the nature of the struggle between them, which was essentially a striving for supreme authority and the perquisites of power, militated against any real composition of the differences between them. Both in word and in deed, the Communists made it clear that it was their intention to overthrow the National Government and to install a regime of their own in its place. The entry of the United States into the war against Japan assured both contestants of an ultimate Japanese defeat, and neither of them thereafter felt it necessary to choose between tolerance of each other and subjugation by Japan.

Position of the Great Powers Prior to 1942

The United States, when it came upon the Far Eastern scene, toward the close of the eighteenth century, sought no special or exclusive privileges and entertained no territorial ambitions. It asked no more than a fair field and no favor, and it acted on this policy from the time of its first treaty with China in 1844.

At the end of the nineteenth century, when China was demonstrably unable to withstand great-power imperialism, the United States proposed (1899) to the governments of France, Great Britain, Germany, Japan, and Russia formal declarations of an "open door" policy with respect to the leased territories and the so-called "spheres of influence" or special interests that these countries were developing in China. A year later, during the Boxer uprising, the United States similarly made formal declaration of the policy of respect for the territorial and administrative integrity of China, since it was reasoned that an independent China was a prerequisite to the preservation of the "open door" and to the maintenance of stability in the Far East.[1]

In 1908 in the Root-Takahira exchange of notes, the governments of the United States and of Japan mutually declared that they were determined to support "by all pacific means at our disposal the independence of China and the principle of equal opportunity for commerce and industry of all nations in that Empire." The most

[1] U. S. Department of State, *United States Relations with China* (August 1949), pp. 414-17.

complete commitment to these principles was given expression in the Nine Power Treaty Regarding China
concluded at the Washington Conference in 1922. In
that treaty the parties other than China pledged themselves "to respect the sovereignty, the independence,
and the territorial and administrative integrity of
China," to provide China opportunity to develop and
maintain for itself an effective and stable government,
to support the principle of equal opportunity for the
commerce of all nations throughout China, and to refrain from seeking special rights or privileges that would
abridge the rights of nationals of friendly states and
from countenancing action inimical to the security of
such states.

When Japan invaded and occupied Manchuria in
1932, Secretary of State Stimson, in identic notes addressed on January 7, 1932, to the Chinese and the Japanese governments, stated that the American Government

... cannot admit the legality of any situation *de facto* nor
does it intend to recognize any treaty or agreement entered
into between those governments [the governments of China
and Japan], or the agents thereof, which may impair the
treaty rights of the United States or its citizens in China,
including those which relate to the sovereignty, the independence, or the territorial and administrative integrity of
the Republic of China, or to the international policy relative
to China, commonly known as the open door policy.

In 1937, after the outbreak of the Sino-Japanese conflict, Secretary of State Hull affirmed clearly that the
American Government considered that the stated principles of its foreign policy were specifically applicable
to situations that might arise from the hostilities then in
progress in China.

Early in 1941 the Japanese Government presented to
the United States Government proposals for an agreement looking to a settlement of problems outstanding

between the two countries in the Pacific area. Secretary of State Hull asked for a definite assurance before entering into a negotiation that the Japanese Government was willing and able to renounce its policies of aggression and to adopt four principles that the United States regarded as fundamental to sound international relations. These principles were:

(1) Respect for the territorial integrity and the sovereignty of each and all nations;
(2) Support of the principle of noninterference in the internal affairs of other countries;
(3) Support of the principle of equality, including equality of commercial opportunity;
(4) Nondisturbance of the *status quo* in the Pacific except as the *status quo* may be altered by peaceful means.

The Secretary assured the Japanese Ambassador that the United States would be willing to consider any proposal that the Japanese Government might offer which would be consistent with these principles.

In the ensuing exploratory conversations, Secretary Hull also made it clear that the United States would not assent to the preferred political and economic position for Japan in China that was implied in the proposals offered by the Japanese. He offered, however, co-operation of the United States in seeking for both countries nondiscriminatory access in the procurement of raw materials in the countries of the southwest Pacific; the negotiation of a trade agreement based on most-favored-nation treatment; and other arrangements which, he thought and said, would give Japan all that its government professed to be seeking in the way of security and economic opportunity. The Japanese answer was an all-out attack on Pearl Harbor and on British, Dutch, and American possessions in the Far East.

For a period of two centuries prior to 1834, British relations with China were concerned almost wholly

with trade, conducted exclusively through the port of
Canton and monopolized by the British East India
Company. In 1834, the company lost its monopoly. The
industrial revolution in England placed great pressure
upon British enterprise to expand its trade with China.
Friction between the British and the Chinese arising
from galling Chinese restrictions on trade, from a refusal to deal with the British on terms of equality, and
from British unwillingness to expose their subjects to
the rigors and arbitrariness of Chinese justice, led in
1839 to the so-called "Opium War." In 1841 the British
occupied Hong Kong, whose cession was confirmed in
the treaty of Nanking a year later. That treaty provided
also for the opening to trade of four ports in addition
to Canton and for the exercise by Great Britain of
extraterritorial rights. Anglo-Chinese difficulties, however, persisted and led again to hostilities in 1856; and
in 1858-60 China was obliged to make further concessions.

The interests of the United Kingdom in China, during most of the period of its relations with that country, have exceeded in importance those of any other
foreign power. These interests have included a flourishing trade, direct investments, amounting just before the
Second World War to $563 million, in shipping, com-
merce, railways, industry, and public utilities, besides
investments of $278 million in Chinese government obli-
gations, and a political interest created by its possession
of Hong Kong, by the propinquity to China of other
British Asian possessions, and by the exigencies of maintaining the British power position in the Far East.

British policy toward China, especially after the turn
of the present century, generally maintained concert
with American policy. From the outset of the all-out

attack on China by Japan in 1937, British interests suffered severely from Japanese acts. Britain, then preoccupied with the crisis and the subsequent war in Europe, deferred largely to the leadership of the United States in efforts to restrain Japan.

Russia, whose policies of expansion in the Far East date from the opening years of the seventeenth century, has the longest and most consistent record of any country for pursuing a course of action antithetical to the traditional principles of United States policy. By 1904 Russia had acquired, in addition to sovereignty over all of continental East Asia north of the Amur and east of the Ussuri and the Tumen rivers, a sphere of influence amounting to a strangle hold in Manchuria. Defeated in 1905 by Japan, Russia was obliged to hand over to the victor the leasehold of the Kwantung peninsula, the railways south of Changchun, and other extensive properties in south Manchuria. From then on until 1918 Tsarist Russian, and thereafter until 1945 Soviet Russian, ambitions in the Far East were held in check by Japanese power rather than by the restraints of international agreements.

Developments During the War

The wartime relations of the United States with China were based on the historical position that has been sketched above. A significant addition was, however, made during the war. The United States desired to assist China not only to wage war effectively against Japan but also to take an active and leading part in sustaining a new structure for world peace. It was realized that China had been a source of general instability in the Far East because its weakness had exposed it to encroachment by predatory powers. In effect, the United States envisaged developments that would cause China to assume a role in which it would replace Japan, when that country had suffered defeat, in the position of foremost influence in the Far East.

In January 1943 the United States concluded a treaty with China for the relinquishment of extraterritorial rights in China and the regulation of related matters. In that treaty the complete sovereign equality of China with the United States was recognized. Shortly thereafter, the United States began to institute efforts to obtain for China recognition as one of the "Big Four"—later Five—powers. At the end of the same year came the Cairo Conference.

Efforts to help make China the leading power in the Far East as well as to make effective its contribution as an ally in the war against Japan encountered practical difficulties. The irresolvable conflict between the National Government and the Chinese Communists lay at the heart of these difficulties. In the American view, this was an especially significant source of trouble, because of its possible repercussions on relations with the Soviet Union.

In June 1944 Vice President Wallace went to China on a special mission for the declared purpose of seeing "what we [the United States] could do toward consolidating the Chinese war effort against Japan." During his visit Mr. Wallace exchanged views with Generalissimo Chiang Kai-shek on the problem of the Chinese Communists and the desirability of improving relations between China and the Soviet Union. The Generalissimo expressed a desire for the assistance of President Roosevelt in these matters. Mr. Wallace's recorded statements reflected an apprehension lest a deterioration of the relations between the National Government and the Chinese Communists lead to a conflict with the Soviet Union.

In September 1944 General Patrick Hurley arrived in China as a special representative of the President of the United States, and some months later, through his efforts with both parties, the National Government and the Chinese Communists entered into negotiations. Although negotiations went on intermittently for nearly two years, first during the mission of General Hurley and later during that of General George Marshall, they finally failed because the objectives of the parties had from the first been irreconcilable, since each side desired a position of dominance in China.

The desire among American military authorities to ensure participation by the Soviet Union in the final operation for the defeat of Japan was one of the principal factors that prompted President Roosevelt at Yalta, in February 1945, to enter into an agreement whereby the Soviet Union undertook to join in the war against Japan and to support in China only the National Government, which was recognized as the legitimate government of China by all of the powers, including the Soviet Union. In return for the Russian pledge thus given, China was to concur in the *status quo* (which the Russians interpreted as the independence) of Outer Mongolia and to assent to the taking by the Soviet Union of a position in Manchuria substantially the same as that enjoyed by Czarist Russia just prior to the Russo-Japanese War of 1904-05. These obligations on the part of China were to be subject to the concurrence of its government (which the President agreed to take measures to obtain). Subsequently, on August 14, 1945, China concluded with the Soviet Union a treaty substantially on the Yalta terms but with some modifications of the original Soviet demands in favor of China and some additional provisions in favor of the Soviet Union. The most significant gains of the Soviet Union in Manchuria under the treaty were control over a naval base at Port Arthur for thirty years, joint and equal Russo-Chinese ownership of the key railways in Manchuria, and a thirty-year lease of half of the port facilities at Dairen.

Postwar Situation Prior to 1949

By the time of the Japanese formal surrender on September 2, 1945, negotiations between the National Government and the Chinese Communists, under American prompting, had seemingly brought about agreement on certain points. This was viewed by some American leaders as warranting an expectation that a peaceful settlement would eventually be reached. Many observers, however, were skeptical of such a possibility, especially in view of the fact that the Communists had taken advantage of the defeat of Japan to occupy various areas from which the Nationalists had been expelled by the Japanese in the course of their invasion. By November little doubt remained of the imminent danger of a resumption of hostilities. The discussions looking toward the maintenance of a truce were deadlocked: the Communists were unwilling to promise not to attack lines of communications unless the Government promised to stop the movement of Nationalist troops into North China. Such a promise the Government flatly refused to give.

Commenting on these developments, the American Embassy at Chungking reported that there was grave danger that widespread civil war might arise out of the stalemate in the truce negotiations between the National Government and the Chinese Communists.

In December 1945 two important steps were taken by the government of the United States. In the first place on the 15th President Truman issued a public statement of United States policy toward China, in which he declared that "it is the firm belief of this Government that a strong, united and democratic China is of the utmost importance to the success" of the United Nations Organization and for world peace. He noted that it was in the most vital interest of the United States and of the United Nations that the people of China should overlook no opportunity to adjust their internal differences by means of peaceful negotiation. He believed it essential that there be arranged a cessation of internal hostilities for completing the return of all China to effective Chinese control and that there be held a national conference of representatives of the major Chinese political elements to develop a solution that would bring about the unification of China. He referred to the fact of international recognition of the National Government as the only legal government of China, which government he said was the proper instrument to achieve the objective of unification. He then went on to say:

The United States is cognizant that the present National Government of China is a 'one-party government' and believes that peace, unity and democratic reform in China will be furthered if the basis of this Government is broadened to include other political elements in the country. Hence, the United States strongly advocates that the national conference of representatives of major political elements in the country agree upon arrangements which would give those elements a fair and effective representation in the Chinese National Government. . . .

As China moves toward peace and unity along the lines

described above, the United States would be prepared to assist the National Government in every reasonable way to rehabilitate the country, improve the agrarian and industrial economy, and establish a military organization capable of discharging China's national and international responsibilities for the maintenance of peace and order. In furtherance of such assistance, it would be prepared to give favorable consideration to Chinese requests for credits and loans under reasonable conditions for projects which would contribute toward the development of a healthy economy throughout China and healthy trade relations between China and the United States.

Following the issuance of this statement, President Truman, as the second step, sent General George C. Marshall to China as his special representative. The General's principal mission was to "bring to bear . . . the influence of the United States" in order that "the unification of China by peaceful, democratic methods be achieved as soon as possible."[2]

Through General Marshall's good offices, a truce was agreed to on January 10, 1946. The respite, however, was only a brief one, for armed clashes soon began again. During 1946, although negotiations went on intermittently, the fighting spread, and the prospects of a peaceful settlement steadily diminished. In the spring of 1947 the National Government decided that there could be no settlement by peaceful means—a decision at which the Chinese Communists had arrived much earlier—and it announced that it would wage "a war to the death" with the Communists.

In the meantime, the National Assembly had adopted in December 1946 a constitution which was to go into effect on December 25, 1947. After the promulgation of the constitution on January 1, 1947, the government invited all political parties and groups to take part in the

[2] The same, p. 605.

principal policy-making branches of the government.
The Democratic Socialist Party and the Youth Party,
which were hardly parties in the American sense, accepted the invitation, but the Democratic League and
the Communists declined the invitation, the latter in-
sisting on a return to military positions as they had been
on January 13, 1946, and on repeal of the constitution. In
April 1947 the National Government announced that
one-party rule in China had come to an end with the
fulfillment of the Kuomintang's promise to hand over
political power to the people, and that the program for
establishing constitutional government had been completed.

After the general election of delegates to the National
Assembly, held on November 21, 1947, it was officially
affirmed that, according to estimates, more than 100
million voters had gone to the polls. When the National
Assembly convened at Nanking on March 28, 1947, it
re-elected Generalissimo Chiang Kai-shek as President
of China and elected General Li Tsung-jen as Vice
President.

The National Government in reality was and for a
long time had been a coalition, united only in the opposition of its components to the Chinese Communists. Its
dominant group, the Kuomintang, had as of May 1948 a
membership of about eight millions. The Kuomintang
leaders included military men, bureaucrats, representatives of the landed gentry, and others. The military leaders had their "private" armies and their civilian supporters, and they had interests wherever sources of patronage,
influence, and revenue could be developed. The para-
mountcy of Chiang Kai-shek was attributable to his per-
sonality, to his skill as a politician, and to his methods.
In all these ways, he gained and kept both votes and con-

trol of the balance of military power, an indispensable basis for exercising supreme political authority under the conditions that prevailed in China.

Despite the key position occupied by military men, some civilian leaders exercised a significant influence. Among civilian groups, the one most strongly entrenched in the bureaucracy was the ultra-conservative "C.C. Clique," so-called because it was headed by two brothers, Ch'en Li-fu and Ch'en Kuo-fu. This group is said to have controlled 30 per cent of the votes in the National Assembly and 50 per cent of the membership of the Legislative Yuan.

A vicious circle in the Chinese internal political situation lay in the fact that while disturbed conditions favored military domination, this domination made for the arbitrary exercise of power and in turn bred turmoil, which prevented the development of national unity and stability. To be sure, there were in the government many officials of outstanding ability and probity. The high caliber of the staff of the Chinese Ministry of Foreign Affairs and the Diplomatic Service has been traditional, but these officials functioned essentially as technicians and exercised little political influence.

Until recently, classical scholars with traditional training were found in large numbers in China's civil service, but gradually the number of such scholars decreased and their places in the service were filled by graduates of modern institutions of learning, at home and abroad, together with relatives, protegés, and henchmen of influential political figures. The rank and file of the service—clerks and scribes—differed hardly at all in their perspectives from their predecessors through the centuries, except that increasing inflation made their salaries progressively more inadequate to provide even a simple livelihood. The bureaucracy on the whole was a repository of the innate conservatism of China and of its glorification of the past. Its power lay in its capacity to obstruct progress. Its weakness lay in its inability to check the political domination of military politicians.

This weakness was increased by the extent to which incompetence and venality prevailed. Chiang Kai-shek himself, on various occasions, berated party leaders for low morale and corruption, and urged the Kuomintang to clear its own house in order to gain popular support. In China, it was common knowledge, that largely as a result of the breakdown in morale following the war and of the sharp decreases in the purchasing power of official salaries, abuses of the traditionally sanctioned and conventionalized practices of the "squeeze" developed. The postwar trend in China toward the nationalization of certain strategic industries and the increase in governmental control over business in general facilitated the development of new and wider applications of the squeeze system.

Incompetence in official positions was further increased by the practice of buying appointments, by the exigencies of a family system that impelled officials to find places for relatives and friends, by a lack of discipline, and by a failure to introduce systematic methods of recruitment, training, and advancement of personnel. After 1928 a good beginning had been made toward reform, but all efforts in that direction were interrupted by the all-out Japanese attack on China in 1937. Much of the subsequent lapsing from the standards then set was attributable to war conditions, and later to wartime inflation. As long as unstable conditions prevailed in the country, it was difficult for the government to take measures to eradicate the fundamental causes of these evils.

The Chinese Civil War

During the course of China's armed resistance to Japan, with industry and trade paralyzed, the National Government was obliged to revert to a political economy based on agricultural land and land rents. But the government, in order to hold the support of the land-owning classes who paid the land tax, favored the landlords to the point of alienating the peasantry, who comprise four fifths of the population. The Chinese Communists were thus afforded opportunity to make capital of peasant disaffection.

The armed conflict between the National Government and the Chinese Communists had been carried on with intermittent truces under the same respective principal leaders since 1927. Between 1937 and 1945, the preoccupation of both sides with resistance against Japanese aggression constituted a deterrent to an all-out armed conflict between them. After V-J day, American good offices to reconcile their differences and to bring about a united China proved ineffective, and recurring armed clashes gradually grew into a full-scale "civil" war. The loss by the Nationalists of Manchuria was attributable to various circumstances, especially the fact that because of insufficient means of transport, they could not bring in adequate forces to take over the areas evacuated by the Russians in April 1946 in time to prevent those areas from being occupied by the Chinese Communists, to whom the Russians left large quantities of arms and equipment surrendered to them by the Japanese.

It is pertinent here to refer to the testimony before the Armed Services and the Foreign Relations Committees of Lieutenant General Albert Wedemeyer, who at the time of the Japanese surrender was in command of American forces in the China theater, and who, foreseeing that the Nationalist forces would lack the strength to recover Manchuria, had proposed the use of American troops there. He said:

> . . . I did submit to the authorities a request for seven divisions, American divisions, to be made available to me immediately after the war, and I intended to employ them in Manchuria, again to preclude unilateral action on the part of the Soviet in that area until the situation stabilized.
> That request was referred to the Commander of the Far East General MacArthur . . . ; and he refused to make them [the divisions requested] available to me; and there were no other divisions made available.
> . . . .
> I would have liked to have been able to take over the arms and the equipment of the defeated Japanese forces, instead of having those arms and equipment available to the Communists; at least, I would have taken them over and made them available to the Chinese Central Government, . . . which my Government recognized at the time, and was supporting as far as I knew.[3]

By March 1948 the Communists were in effective control of Manchuria.

By the end of 1948 the Communists controlled nearly all the area north of the Yangtze River. The Nationalists suffered a serious defeat at Hsuchow; and the collapse of the "gold yuan" currency introduced in August disrupted economic activity and created widespread distress and demoralization among the middle class. In January 1949 the Communists, soon after their capture

[3] *Military Situation in the Far East,* Hearings before the Senate Committee on Armed Services and the Committee on Foreign Relations, 82 Cong., 1 sess. (1951), p. 2415.

of Peiping and Tientsin, announced the terms on which they would be willing to negotiate for a settlement. These terms were in effect a demand for complete surrender. Within a week the National Government announced the transfer of the capital from Nanking to Canton, and Chiang Kai-shek announced his voluntary retirement as President and left Nanking. Chiang did not, however, relinquish his control of various units of the Nationalist fighting forces, including the Air Force, or of the Government's specie reserves, which were transferred to Formosa over a period of months between late 1948 and early 1949. On January 21, 1949 Vice President Li Tsung-jen was installed as Acting President.

On January 25 the Chinese Communist radio announced that the Communists were willing to commence peace negotiations with the five Nationalist negotiators whose appointment for that purpose had been disclosed a few days earlier. The Communists insisted, however, upon the terms previously announced and upon Li's turning over to them forthwith, as an indication of his "sincerity," a number of alleged "war criminals," including Chiang Kai-shek.

Notwithstanding the unpromising prospects for a negotiated agreement, a Nationalist peace delegation left for Peiping on April 1, and, according to a Communist broadcast, formal negotiations were begun after a twelve-day period of informal interchanges of views. Chiang Kai-shek's retention of control of the Air Force, of many of the best troops, and of the specie reserve impaired the bargaining power of the National Government. The Nationalist delegation was reported to have been presented with a draft agreement, which they were given until April 20 to sign. The draft was said to include four fundamental demands, namely: (1) unopposed crossing of the Yangtze River by Communist armies, at ten specified points; (2) reorganization of the Nationalist Army into the Communist "People's Liberation Army"; (3) immediate Communist absorption of the Yangtze River region and the eventual Communist occupation of the whole of China; and (4) temporary continuance of Nationalist authority in Kuomintang areas on a "caretaker" basis pending convocation of a political consultative conference to establish a Communist-dominated coalition government. The Nationalists rejected those demands and negotiations were broken off.

The Communist armies, which had been for two months consolidating their positions along the north bank of the Yangtze River, then began a movement to cross the river at points along a 600-mile stretch. Chiang Kai-shek failed to commit the Air Force and his best ground troops to the defense of the Yangtze River line, and the crossings, which might have been made costly to the Communists, were effected with ease. Nanking was abandoned by the Nationalists without serious fighting on April 24, and on May 27 the Communists took over Shanghai.

The military operations of the Nationalists that were perhaps the most damaging to the Communists were the activities of the Navy and the Air Force against interport traffic and foreign commerce. These operations, in so far as they were carried out against foreign vessels, together with the warnings issued by the National Government that ports in the Communist-held areas were to be closed, evoked strong protests from the British and the United States governments. Nothwithstanding these protests, attacks on British and American ships continued to occur even outside of Chinese territorial waters, with the result that the British in some cases provided their merchant vessels with naval escorts.

Defeat and Flight of the National Government

Early in October the Nationalists gave up Canton without a serious struggle, having first moved their capital to Chungking. By the end of November they abandoned Chungking and shifted the capital to Chengtu. General Pai Chung-hsi, who had been expected to put up a good fight to prevent invasion by the Communists of his native province of Kwangsi, fell back with his command, reportedly because he could not get the funds to make the payments that had been due his troops for two months. On November 20 Acting President Li flew to Hong Kong and entered a hospital for the announced purpose of receiving treatment for stomach ulcers. Subsequently, he came to New York and he is still, as of October 1, 1952, in the United States. In December 1949 the Nationalists abandoned Chengtu, and the National Government withdrew from the mainland to Formosa and made Taipei its capital.

Observers have offered a variety of explanations to account for the continuance during the postwar period of the progressive deterioration of the National Government and the accelerating pace of the crumbling during 1948 and 1949 of its resistance to the Chinese Communists. It will be useful to turn attention to the underlying factors, for the conclusions reached in regard thereto may affect significantly the course of future policy toward China of the United States and of the other democracies.

The Chinese classics have taught that the Emperor ruled by the mandate of Heaven; that if he failed to rule with virtue, he forfeited this mandate; and that, in these circumstances, the people are justified in revolting. Some observers have attempted to explain the defeat of the National Government by reference to this doctrine. Such an explanation implies that there was a revolt, a successful revolt, of and by the people—which there was not. It is true that the people had lost confidence in the devotion of the National Government to their welfare and in its capacity to extricate the nation from the grave problems that beset it after eight long years of resistance to Japan. The articulate public had either become lukewarm in its support of the National Government or apathetic to the point of adopting an attitude of neutrality as between the Kuomintang and the Communists. Enthusiasm for the latter, however, was largely confined to student groups and to a section of the intellectuals. It is therefore inaccurate to describe the triumph of the Communists on the mainland as a successful popular revolution. Rather, the triumph has been that of a power group possessed of superior organization, discipline, and determination, more efficient and more ruthless than the government (also a power group), which it attacked.

Long before Pearl Harbor, when the United States was brought into the Pacific war, the power and the prestige of the National Government of China had been seriously impaired by the struggle with Japan. By 1941 the Communists had consequently considerably expanded the area of China over which they exercised *de facto* control.

The eventual defeat of the Nationalists at the hands of the Communists is also in no small part attributable to the physical and moral "beating" which both Government and people suffered during eight years at the hands of the Japanese. The plans and efforts of the National

Government for constructive development were brought to an abrupt end by the general assault that the Japanese began in 1937. When in 1945 Japan was defeated and its forces were withdrawn from the areas in China that they had occupied, there was created a physical, political, and economic vacuum that the weakened National Government was not able to fill. The Communist armed opposition was able, with the covert assistance of the Soviet Union, to take advantage of that situation—and it did so, very effectively.

The Chinese Communist leaders craftily deferred revelation of the full scope of their program of "reforms" and the methods which they proposed to employ in putting their program through until they had consolidated their control over the country. Many of the policies and practices of the Communist regime—especially those that run counter to the integrity of the Chinese family system, their respect for private property, and the tradition of noninterference by the state with the normal every day life of the people—are distasteful to most Chinese. Much of the counter-Communist guerrilla activity that was once reported to be widespread, especially in South China, was attributable to disaffection over the innovations and the "security" measures that the Communists were trying to impose by force. The mass executions and all sorts of "purgings" to which the Communists have resorted are believed to have largely stamped out such counter-revolutionary activity. This may with warrant be regarded as evidence of Communist strength rather than of popular reconciliation to communism.

Perhaps a more reliable indication of Chinese sentiment, in view of the difficulty of verifying reports of what is going on within China, is afforded by the prevailing attitudes among the ten million and more Chinese overseas. In the countries of southeast Asia, where the overwhelming majority of these Chinese have settled, the Chinese residents, who two or three years ago were divided in their allegiance, are reliably reported to have been veering in ever-increasing numbers to the support of the National Government. Most of these overseas Chinese have been unfavorably impressed by the campaign under way in China for the destruction of the so-called "capitalist" class. Again, the overseas Chinese have no sympathy with the Communist policy of aggression in Korea, which they consider not in the interest of the Chinese people. Nor do the Chinese abroad feel anything but contempt for the Communist regime on account of the practice it has instituted of extorting money from them by threatening the well-being and the lives of the members of their families held as hostages in China.[4]

Conflict Between United States and Soviet Objectives

In the document entitled *United States Relations with China,* issued by the Department of State on August 5, 1949, there is described in much detail the development of United States policy toward China during and after the Second World War. It is pertinent to note that

[4] This reported growing revulsion among the Chinese people does not necessarily imply a corresponding change in the attitude toward Chiang Kai-shek and the Kuomintang from one of disapproval, disappointment or apathy to one of enthusiasm. To many modern-minded Chinese liberals, Chiang is the embodiment of an outmoded political order that seeks to hold power not through providing beneficent administration but by placing personal adherents in key positions and dispensing patronage in their favor. The choice that many of these liberals now make in favor of Chiang in preference to Communism represents no more than a reconciliation, in the absence of a practical third alternative, to what they consider the lesser of two evils.

in mid-1949 the United States Government considered that it was confronted with grave difficulties in carrying out its declared policy with respect to China. These difficulties were stated to be: the fact that a large proportion of the military supplies furnished to the Chinese armies by the United States since V-J day had fallen into the hands of the Communists through the military ineptitude of the Nationalist leaders, their defections and their surrenders; absence in the Nationalist forces of a will to fight; the fact that the key areas of China were now in the hands of the Communists, who had publicly recognized the leadership of Russia, a country which under Tzars and Communists alike had tried to extend its control in the Far East; and that, although United States aid in the past had helped the Chinese to resist foreign aggression, in this case, "the foreign domination has been masked behind the façade of a vast crusading movement which apparently has seemed to many Chinese to be wholly indigenous and national."[5]

The "letter of transmittal" under which this document was forwarded to the President by the Secretary of State enumerated five basic principles by which the United States would continue to be guided in the new circumstances. These were: (1) encouragement of the development of China as an independent and stable nation; (2) support of the creation of conditions in China that would safeguard basic rights and liberties and promote the well-being of its people; (3) opposition to the subjugation or dismemberment of China by a foreign power or by a regime acting in the interests of such power; (4) continued consultation with the other inter-

---

[5] U. S. Department of State, *United States Relations with China*, p. xvi.

ested powers on measures that would contribute to the welfare and security of the people of the Far East; and (5) encouragement and support of efforts by the United Nations to achieve these objectives and particularly to maintain peace and security in the Far East. The intention was also expressed of continuing to base policy upon "our respect for the Charter [of the United Nations], our friendship for China, and our traditional support for the Open door and for China's independence and administrative and territorial integrity."[6]

The contents of the "letter of transmittal" were explicit as regards certain general aims. No reference was made therein, however, to China as a possible stabilizing force in the Far East. On the contrary, and inferentially, a statement that no further aid was to be extended to the National Government in its efforts to maintain its authority against Communist attack indicated an abandonment of that concept. While notice was served that if the Communist regime in China extended its aggressions beyond China collective action might be sought, the United States Government had in effect written off China as a link in a chain of defense extending across Europe and Asia in favor of a withdrawal, as far as eastern Asia was concerned, to a position on the perimeter of China.

The defeat of Japan in 1945 had created an important power vacuum in the area. The United States was politically unprepared and the National Government of China was unable to fill this vacuum. The Soviet Union was not only prepared to take action, but actually did so. The provisions of the Yalta Agreement and the military arrangements under which the Japanese armies in Manchuria and in Korea north of the thirty-eighth parallel

[6] The same, p. xvii.

were to surrender to Soviet forces lent themselves to this
purpose.

The Soviet Government failed to live up to its commitments under the Yalta Agreement and under the
Sino-Soviet Treaty of 1945. It facilitated the consolidation of Chinese Communist power in Manchuria. When
the Chinese Communists, thus strengthened, succeeded
in overrunning the key areas of China proper and announced in October 1949 the establishment of a Central
People's Government of the People's Republic of China,
the Soviet Government promptly accorded that government recognition as the government of China, and four
months later, in February 1950, concluded with it an
offensive and defensive alliance. Since then, the Soviet
Union has consistently supported the Chinese Communist regime in extending and consolidating its authority
in China, in making its power and influence felt elsewhere in the Far East—in Korea and Indo-China, for
example—and in its effort to gain international recognition and especially to replace the National Government
in the United Nations.

It is thus evident that there is a sharp and basic conflict in the Far East between the interests, objectives, and
policies of the United States and those of the Soviet
Union. It is the declared policy of the United States to
foster there, as elsewhere, the development of free political institutions. The Soviet Union professes to have similar objectives, but its action, in relation especially to
adjacent countries, indicates that its real objective is the
establishment of Communist domination, if not Soviet
control. The United States seeks to gain its ends through
constructive efforts to promote economic and political
stability and progress everywhere, in the belief that such
a course will ensure its own well-being and national

and world security. The Soviet Union employs tactics that seem to be largely obstructive, and apparently believes that the weakening of the smaller nations that it does not already control will facilitate the spread of communism and of Soviet influence. In these senses, conflict in the Far East has become part of a similar conflict in Europe and elsewhere.

The broad pattern of developments that has been sketched is relevant to an examination of the position of the United States with respect to Formosa. The simple fact of the successful transfer of the National Government of China to a relatively secure island base has had the effect of bringing this larger pattern of conflict to a focal point. It had of course been evident from the outset that the conflicts of interests were not susceptible of being easily resolved. But after the Communist aggression in Korea, one clear objective of which was to checkmate the emergence of Japan as a factor in the efforts of the free world to stem the advance of militant Communism in Asia, it was inevitable that American public opinion should sense the implications of the Communist move and should become more firmly insistent upon the according of American support to the National Government of China. Thus the difficulties of the situation were immeasurably intensified. The three following chapters deal with the changes in attitude and with the sequence of events from 1950 to the present time.

CHAPTER 6.

Formosa As the Seat of the National Government

WITH the removal to Formosa of the seat of the National Government, two governmental mechanisms became established on the island. Formosa continued to be a province of China, with its own provincial government. But this government now had to operate side by side with the National Government. It is therefore necessary to describe briefly the organization of both governments and their relation to each other. It is also necessary to examine the economic situation in Formosa as it relates to the operation of both governments.

Organization of the National Government

When the National Government of China established itself in Formosa in December 1949, the political system that was put into operation followed generally the patterns that had been evolved on the mainland. Notwithstanding the fact that the dictatorship of the Kuomintang was declared at an end in April 1947, the party continued to be the predominant force in the functioning of the National Government. The Kuomintang was organized vertically to comprise a national congress and four descending regional bodies: the provincial councils, the county (hsien) councils, the district (chu) councils, and the subdistrict councils.[1] The supreme authority of the National Party Congress was vested in the party chief, Chiang Kai-shek, who is ex-officio chairman of the Congress.

Formerly, there were three bodies under the National Party Congress to which power was delegated: the Central Executive Committee, under the chairmanship of Chiang Kai-shek, which was the chief policy-forming organ of the party and of the Government; the Central Supervisory Committee, a sort of board of review; and the Central Political Council (abolished during the war). In 1950 the organization of the party was greatly simplified and made more compact. This development was doubtless facilitated by the progressive thinning out of party members during the year or two before the exodus to Formosa, and by the absence of many who failed to find their way there.

These changes made possible the tightening of Chiang Kai-shek's political control. The Central Executive Committee and the Central Supervisory Committee were abolished in June 1950 and were replaced respectively by a Central Reform Committee and a Central Consultative Committee. Only the first of these, with a membership of 16, chiefly key figures in the party, is important. That Committee is charged with reshaping party policy. Party influences independent of Chiang Kai-shek are declining. The power of the "C.C.Clique," for example, is waning, but in view of the ultra-conservatism of that group this may be not unfortunate. At the same time, the rank and file of the party members are reported to have become dispirited over their apparent

[1] Of the provincial councils, only the one in Formosa has been functioning since the abandonment of the mainland.

impotence, and this bodes ill for the future prospects of infusing the leadership with new blood.

Like that of the Kuomintang, the structure of the government also underwent some streamlining. There was a considerable amount of consolidation and re-organization of departments and bureaus, together with a redistribution of functions. Of the 3,000 members elected in 1947 to the National Assembly, only about 1,200 are in Formosa. That body, however, had not become a significant factor in the political life of China. The Office of the President (Tsungtungfu) is the supreme organ of the National Government, and the Executive Yuan is the highest administrative organ. The latter body comprises eight ministries, two commissions, and a varying number of independent bureaus. There are also a number of ministers without portfolio.

Chiang Kai-shek has a three-fold position. He is the party chief of the Kuomintang, the President of the National Government, a position that he resumed in March 1950, and the commander in chief of the armed forces. The sources of his power are the armed forces, the national purse, and the secret police, which he controls. Chiang's dictatorial authority is not founded on law but is maintained through political manipulation and the dispensation of patronage, which enables him to hold the personal loyalty of persons whom he places in key positions and to keep the opposition ineffective and disunited. It is of course much easier to keep tight control of power in a small area such as that of Formosa than in the sprawling expanse of the Chinese mainland.

The political figures closest to Chiang are his wife, Mei-ling; his son, Chiang Ching-kuo, who holds a number of offices concurrently; General Chou Chih-jou, Chief of Staff of the Army; General Chang Chung, a former Prime Minister; General T'ang En-po, who commands an important secret police body as well as certain army units; Ch'en Ch'eng, the President of the Executive Yuan (a position corresponding to that of prime minister); Wu Te-chen, a roving ambassador, who is especially influential with overseas Chinese; Wang Shih-chieh, formerly Foreign Minister and now Secretary-General of the office of the President; and a few ex-war lords.

The chain of army command runs theoretically from Generalissimo Chiang Kai-shek through the Executive Yuan to the Minister of Defense and thence through the Chief of Staff, Chou Chih-jou, to the field commanders. Actually, the chain runs directly from the Generalissimo to Chou Chih-jou. General Sun Li-jen, titular commander in chief of the Army, though perhaps the most competent general in the Nationalist army, has little power. There are under his direct command only some 25,000 training troops. The defense area commanders are controlled either directly by the Generalissimo or by Chou Chih-jou, Ch'en Ch'eng, or T'ang En-po. Similarly, the chain of command in the Navy runs from Chiang Kai-shek to the naval commander in chief, Admiral Ma Chi-chuang, and thence to the heads of all naval activities; and the Air Force chain of command, from the Generalissimo to Wang Shou-ming commander in chief of the Air Force.

General MacArthur, in his testimony before the Senate committees on Armed Services and on Foreign Relations on May 3, 1951, described his impressions of the military establishment of the National Government in Formosa, as derived during his visit there in August 1950. His account of these impressions may be summarized as follows: There were probably some 500,000 troops, capable of being made into an excellent force. Their personnel was good and their morale high. Material equipment varied in quality and was deficient in artillery, trucks, and in a great many modern refinements. The Nationalists probably had between 200 and 250 planes, and their pilots were "rather good." The navy was only a conglomeration of small ships, which looked smart but were capable merely of small coastal activities. If properly equipped, the troops would probably be in as good shape as would be possible without combat experience.[2]

Organization of the Taiwan Provincial Government

With the transfer of the National Government from the mainland to Formosa in December 1949, the Chairman of the Provincial Council, General Ch'en Ch'eng, was elevated to the presidency of the Executive Yuan. He was replaced in the chairmanship of the Provincial Government by Mr. K. C. Wu, who had, as Mayor of Shanghai, established among the modern-minded Chinese and the American residents of that city a reputation for progressiveness and efficiency.

The Provincial Government, as reorganized in 1949, is composed of a Provincial Council of 23 commissioners, among whom are the heads of the various departmental units as ex-officio members. Seventeen of the commissioners are native Formosans. Administrative functions are grouped into ten departments: Civil Affairs, Finance, Reconstruction, Education, Agriculture and Forestry, Social Affairs, Police Affairs, Communica-

[2] *Military Situation in the Far East,* Hearings before the Senate Committee on Armed Services and the Committee on Foreign Relations, 82 Cong. 1 sess. (1951), p. 23.

tions, Public Health, and the Food Bureau. There is also a Provincial Assembly, which has no legislative power but which can make recommendations, hear reports, and interpellate officials of the Provincial Government. The powers of the Assembly are circumscribed by provisions which require that its acts must not be in contravention of national laws and regulations, and that in case of a dispute between the Assembly and the Provincial Council the National Government shall decide.[3]

For purposes of local administration, the island has now been reorganized into five independent municipalities and 16 counties (hsien). The councils for these 21 units of local administration are to be elected by secret ballot. These councils are in turn to elect the members of the Provincial Assembly.

Separate and special arrangements have been made for the administration of the mountain areas that are inhabited by the as yet unassimilated aboriginal tribesmen, whose number as of 1949 was placed at 91,000 (out of a total of 140,500 aborigines). After the Chinese reoccupation of Formosa, general jurisdiction over these areas was shifted from the Police Department to the Department of Civil Affairs, but responsibility for educational matters and for health was taken over respectively by the Department of Education and the Department of Public Health. Thirty communes have been demarcated, each having a popularly elected mountain tribesman as a head, but assisted by a lowlander as an executive secretary. The executive secretary is appointed by the magistrate of the county in which the commune is located. Each commune is entitled to elect one representative on the county council, which would mean an average of one per 3,000 of the mountain population,

[3] Han Lih-wu, *Taiwan Today* (Taipei, 1951).

whereas the average for the general population is one
per 10,000 of the population. The aborigines are also
given representation in the Provincial Assembly. One
tribesman serves as a commissioner, representing all the
tribes and tribesmen, in the Provincial Council. In the
160 elementary schools provided for the aborigines,
17,000 students are enrolled.

All of this suggests improvement in many respects
over the situation that existed when the Chinese took
possession from the Japanese. However, the deterioration in the economic situation of the aborigines that set
in during the war has not yet been wholly overcome.
The area under cultivation by them is still about 20 per
cent less than it was in prewar years, being placed at
about 90,000 acres, or one acre per tribesman.[4]

The personnel in all ranks of the Formosan provincial
civil service as of the end of June 1950 was 81,006, of
whom 34.5 per cent were mainland Chinese and 65.5
Formosans. At the end of the Japanese administration in
1945, the aggregate personnel in the civil service of the
Government General had been 84,995, of whom 44.5 per
cent were Japanese and 55.5 per cent Formosans. In
1950 out of 8,604 employees in the two higher grades of
the civil service, nearly 60 per cent were Formosans;
whereas under Japanese rule in 1945, out of 2,336 employees only 2 per cent had been Formosans.[5]

The budget estimates of the Provincial Government
for 1951 call for an expenditure of 358.7 million Taipi,
of which 30 per cent is allocated to reconstruction, 23.4
per cent to education, 16 per cent to subsidies, and the
remainder to other administrative and miscellaneous
purposes, and to a reserve fund. The revenues to meet

[4] The same, pp. 40-41.
[5] The same, table p. 30.

these expenditures are to be derived from taxes, monopoly sales of alcoholic beverages and cigarettes, sale
of government properties (chiefly ex-Japanese properties), and profits or income from public enterprises.

In the field of education, the task of the Provincial
Government has been to convert a Japanese system of
education, with a curriculum conducted in the Japanese
language, into a Chinese system. It was necessary to replace the Japanese teaching staffs largely with instructors from the mainland, for there were few Formosans,
who, though they customarily used the dialects of south
China as their spoken medium, were capable of using
standard Chinese as a literary medium. However, the
authorities did not have to start entirely from scratch,
since elementary education under Japanese rule had
been almost universal and since the Japanese written
langauge is based on Chinese characters. Consequently,
the Formosan students were at the outset familiar with
the Chinese ideographs, though they pronounced them
differently and though many ideographs have undergone
in Japanese usage changes in meaning. Perhaps even
more important than the language problem was the
problem of reorienting students from an essentially
Japanese to a Chinese point of view.

By the spring of 1950, there was an enrollment in
elementary schools of nearly 900,000 pupils, or approximately 80 per cent of the school-age population. Upon
completion of a course of study of six years in elementary schools, the pupils are eligible to enter a secondary
school, of which there were in the 1949-50 school year
206, with an enrollment of 115,000.

After the Chinese reoccupation, the Taiwan Imperial
University was renamed the National Taiwan University, and the other three schools of higher education that

provided specialized technical or professional training were either amalgamated with or raised to the status of a college of the university. There has been established also a teachers' college and a college of engineering. All these institutions, except the university itself, which is under the Ministry of Education of the National Government, are under the control of the Provincial Government. In 1949 there were 5,940 students enrolled in schools of college grade, including the university, of whom 2,374 were students from the mainland. The provincial library at Taipei has a collection of 250,000 volumes. Three fifths of them are works in the Japanese language. There are two other provincial libraries and eight municipal and six county libraries, all of them small.

In the field of public health, mention has already been made of the deterioration in public health standards in the initial two years of Chinese administration. Subsequently, there has been an improvement, especially in making provision for physicians to replace the Japanese physicians repatriated in 1945 and in the rehabilitation of the hospitals. It is stated that cholera, bubonic plague, and small pox have disappeared, but that typhoid and diphtheria still remain to be effectively dealt with. The 270 health stations, under the direction of health institutes, are contributing to the promotion of general health. In 1949 a Provincial Malaria Research Institute was established, together with 128 malaria prevention stations. Certain sanitary measures, such as garbage collection and sewage disposal, are admittedly still not up to the standards that were established by the Japanese.[6]

In 1949 the Provincial Government revived the policy

[6] The subject of rural land reform is discussed in Chap. 7, pp. 137-39.

of forest conservation that had been practiced by the Japanese in the prewar years but had been neglected during and after the war. Cutting of forest trees is to be restricted to an amount not exceeding the extent of new forestation. All profits from government logging operations are to be devoted to forestation. Considerable effort has also been devoted to the rehabilitation of the animal husbandry industry and fisheries, which fell on evil days during the war.

Relations Between the National and the Provincial Governments

The fact that the Provincial Government is not autonomous but is under the close control of the National Government has been a handicap to Chairman Wu's efforts to introduce sweeping reforms of a constructive character. It is, however, the declared purpose of the National Government eventually to grant the Province self-rule, the reason given for delay being the threat of a Communist invasion. There is reported to be personal friction between Wu and Ch'en Ch'eng, which manifests itself especially in conflicts over fiscal and economic matters. Moreover, a certain amount of friction would appear to be inevitable in view of the fact that all of the departments of the National Government, except the Ministry of Foreign Affairs and the Ministry of Defense, have functions that overlap those of the Provincial Government.

The Provincial Government is saddled with responsibility for the island's economy but does not control many of the major industries. A National Resources Commission has been given operating control and joint ownership with the Provincial Government of the major

industries requiring technical skills. These include met-
als and minerals enterprises. The National Resources
Commission has been drawing up ambitious programs
for expansion of these industries without regard to the
need for employing available resources in the most ap-
propriate way. The competing requirements of government enterprises operating in this way constitute a major
source of inflationary pressure. Other state-operated
economic enterprises, except the Salt Administration,
have, however, been turned over to the Provincial Government.

The achievements of the Provincial Government in
the fields in which it has been able to exercise a free
hand is in marked contrast to the poor showing made
by the National Government in its efforts on the mainland to eradicate the evils that contributed to its down-
fall. These achievements are impressive when account
is taken of the burden on the island's economy of having
to maintain the National Government, with its war
establishment, and to make provision for a million or
so refugees—responsibilities over which the Provincial
Government has no control but which it cannot escape.

The Provincial Government collects not only the
taxes appertaining to its own budget but also those, with
the exception of the sale and customs receipts, that are
reserved for the National Treasury. The collection of
taxes by the Provincial Government in 1950 through
October amounted to over 194 million Taipi. So far, the
Provincial Government, despite the defense contributions it has made to the National Government, has been
able to balance its budget, although the same is not true
of the National Government.

In 1950 the tax system was simplified and rationalized,
with an eye also to making more equitable the burden

of taxation, a somewhat difficult problem in Formosa, as it is in most countries where it is the practice to rely more largely upon indirect than upon direct taxation. Local government revenues are largely derived from business licenses of various kinds and from taxes upon households, the largest single item being the abattoir tax. Total collections of taxes during the first nine months of 1950 amounted to nearly 54 million Taipi.[7]

The Bank of Taiwan, which was taken over from the Japanese in 1945, serves as a central bank. It issues currency notes, supplies foreign exchange, and acts as the fiscal agent both of the National and of the Provincial Governments. It also serves as a general commercial bank, and has 29 branches. When the Taipi was established as the monetary unit in June 1949, the issue of notes was given a maximum limit of 200 millions, equivalent to $40 million United States currency at the official rate at that time of 5 to 1. The note issue was backed 100 per cent with reserves in gold and in foreign exchange. Subsequently, to meet urgent requirements, notes of a denomination of 50 cents were issued, in addition to coinage, to an amount not exceeding 50 million Taipi. Later, in June 1950, there was a fiduciary issue of a like amount. The total note issue as of October 1950 was 263,124,033 Taipi. In addition to the Bank of Taiwan there are five other provincial banks, each with numerous branches. Bank loans outstanding in October 1950 were just under one million Taipi, of which 90 per cent were loans by the Bank of Taiwan.

Economic Position

Although Formosa is exceptionally productive, the addition to its already dense population of some one

[7] Han Lih-wu, *Taiwan Today,* Chap. 3

million refugees from the Chinese mainland, together
with the expense of maintaining the national defense
establishment, has placed an inordinate burden on the
economy of the island. In 1950 more than 60 per cent
of the expenditures of the central government were for
military purposes. The budget figures, however, do not
include expenditures for imported supplies and equipment, which were paid for out of proceeds from the sale
of assets abroad owned by the National Government.
The civilian expenditures of the National Government,
including those for the upkeep of the Secret Police, are
estimated at about 150 million Taipi (Taiwan currency,
which in 1949 was pegged to United States currency at
the rate of five Taipi to the dollar).

On the revenue side, there was an improvement in
1950 over the previous year, made possible largely by
the boosting of tax rates and more effective suppression
of smuggling. Nevertheless, current revenues were sufficient to meet only about two thirds of government expenditures. These revenues include normal taxes, special
defense taxes, and the sale of "patriotic bonds" and "saving coupons." The last two of these items, which are
estimated to yield 100 million Taipi, are in the nature
of an indiscriminate levy on the public, since the people
are compelled to buy the bonds and the coupons. Tax
revenues are in the neighborhood of 20 per cent of the
national income, which represents a heavy burden on a
territory with such modest resources as Formosa. The
resulting deficit has to be met by the sale of gold and
foreign exchange reserves and of government property,
especially former Japanese residential property; by applying local currency funds derived from the sales proceeds of ECA-financed imports; and, to a smaller extent,
by the expansion of note issues and bank credit. About

35 per cent of the imports are financed through the ECA, and an additional 12 per cent through private use of gold purchased from the government. These funds, added to receipts from exports, have been sufficient to finance essential imports.

With the introduction of the Taipi as the monetary unit, the Formosan Provincial Government, with the support of the National Government, committed itself to a noninflationary program calling for the establishment of a ceiling on note issues. So far, this has been reasonably successful. However, although an inflationary crisis was avoided in 1950, domestic price levels have been rising, owing in part to world price trends and in part to increased rates of taxation. During the second half of 1950, the wholesale price index advanced 40 per cent. Black market interest rates have been as high as 15 per cent monthly, with only a negligible amount of credit available through legitimate channels. These indications reflect the presence of a constant threat to economic stability.

The relative stability of the Taipi in 1950 was attributable to substantial releases of gold and foreign exchange. These releases, however, made possible a flight of capital in great volume. When as a remedial action the government at the end of the year tightened the foreign exchange regulations and suspended the sale of gold, there was a sharp decline in the exchange quotations of Formosan currency. At that time the outlook with regard to the financial condition of the Government in the coming year was not promising, since there appeared slight prospect of reducing expenditures or of increasing revenues. On June 20, 1951, however, additional funds amounting to $41.7 million were made available by the Economic Cooperation Administration for aid to Formosa, and in the autumn the Chinese Government put into force measures that were effective in tightening control of expenditures and in substantially increasing tax revenues. As a result, the financial position of the Government in Formosa was greatly strengthened. Moreover, although there was a poor sugar crop, the drop in sugar exports was almost wholly compensated for by increased exports of other products, notably rice, tea, and bananas.

A previous chapter contained a description of the development of Formosa by Japan, in prewar years, to a high degree of productivity. During the war the island suffered a severe setback. It had to contribute substantially, though indirectly, to the Japanese war effort. Agriculture was crippled by the lack of commercial fertilizers, insecticides, and fungicides, by a diversion of land utilization from normal crops to crops for feeding the Japanese armies, and by difficulties in replacing equipment on large-scale plantations. Industry except as it related to war, languished, and allied bombings caused widespread destruction of industrial plants and disruption of the communications and transportation systems. Commerce slumped, and the financial structure was shaken. In addition, during the 18 months following the Chinese reoccupation in 1945, the island was systematically plundered by Chen Yi's carpetbag administration.

From the low point to which the economy of the island was thus reduced, there has been considerable but uneven improvement. Agricultural employment now represents 66 per cent of total employment, a rather low percentage for Asia. In the 1950-51 crop year, agricultural production had reached an estimated 81 per cent of the 1938 figure. The milled rice output of

1,238,000 metric tons actually surpassed the figure of the prewar peak year. But sugar production in 1950 was only a little over half that of 1938, and the 1951 sugar crop showed a sharp decline from the 1950 figure. This decline was largely compensated for by increases in other crop yields. Certain minor manufacturing industries, notably cotton yarns and cloths, chemicals, cement, and refined petroleum products have, however, made substantial gains over prewar years. Production of aluminum in 1950 amounted to 1,821 tons.

Large-scale industry is concentrated in the hands of 18 public trusts, operated either by the National Government or by the Provincial Government, or by the two jointly. These are as follows:

Operated by the National Government:

Chinese Petroleum Corporation
Taiwan Alumium Works
Taiwan Gold and Copper Mining
   Administration

Chinese Salt Corporation
Hsinchu Coal Mining Administration
Taiwan Steel Works

Operated jointly by the National and the Provincial Governments:

Taiwan Power Company
Taiwan Sugar Corporation
Taiwan Fertilizer Company
Taiwan Cement Corporation

Taiwan Alkali Company
Taiwan Paper and Pulp Corporation
Taiwan Shipbuilding Company
Taiwan Machinery Manufacturing
   Corp.

Operated by the Provincial Government:

Taiwan Industry and Mining Corporation
Taiwan Camphor Bureau

Taiwan Tobacco and Wine Monopoly
Taiwan Agricultural and Forestry
   Development Corporation

Economic assistance from the United States for the rehabilitation and expansion of productive industry and the improvement of transportation facilities has contributed enormously to the maintenance of economic and political stability in Formosa. The Economic Cooperation Administration has furnished commodities needed to keep industries going, to meet urgent civilian requirements, and to yield local currency for specific government needs.

The total exports of Formosa in 1951 were valued at $98.2 million, as compared with $72.4 million in 1950. The total imports—excluding outside aid, chiefly American, were valued at $81.1 million in 1951, as compared with $91.6 million during the previous year. In 1937 and 1938 exports had amounted respectively to $126.7 and $129.9 million and imports to $92.6 and $104.3 million. Thus, although Formosa had not regained its prewar trade position, the extent of recovery in the face of unusual and discouraging conditions warrants optimism for the future. In those two prewar years, well over 90 per cent of Formosan exports were to Japan, and, with the exception of Hong Kong, China, and the Kwantung Leased Territory, no other one importing area took as much as one per cent of its exports. In 1951 Japan, which had in 1950 again appeared in the lead, took 48.3 per cent of Formosan exports, with Hong Kong, the Malay Federation, and the United States next in order, their percentages being 14.8, 10.5, and 5.9, respectively. In 1937 Japan had furnished 86.2 per cent and in 1938 90.0 per cent of Formosan imports. In 1951, if ECA aid and military imports are not included, Japan furnished 48.5 per cent of the imports, followed by the United States, Hong Kong, and the United Kingdom, which furnished 16.5, 13.1, and 3.7 per cent respectively. It should be noted, however, that a substantial part of the prewar trade of Formosa credited to Japan originated from or had its ultimate destination in other countries.

Exports of the principal commodities from Formosa in 1950 compared with those of the years 1937 and 1938 are shown in the table on page 113.

EXPORTS OF PRINCIPAL COMMODITIES FROM FORMOSA

(Quantities in thousands of metric tons, values in millions of dollars)

Item	Quantities				Values			
	1937	1939	1950	1951	1937	1938	1950	1951
Sugar	830	903	608	284	55.1	62.8	54.0[a]	56.3[a]
Rice	312	294	37.3	84.9	36.3	36.1	3.4	13.0
Tea	10	10	7.5	11.2	3.5	3.4	3.2	6.6
Bananas	157	133	12	26.5	3.6	4.4	1.5	3.4
Citronella oil					—	—	—[b]	3.3
Salt					0.4	0.5	0.2	2.8
Pineapples, canned ..					2.7	3.5	0.6	1.8
Camphor, camphor oil					1.8	1.8	2.6	1.5
Alcohol					2.2	4.3	—	—

[a] The figures for the dollar values of sugar exports in 1950 and 1951 of the Taiwan Customs, which are the figures shown in this table, show a marked discrepancy with the Bank of Taiwan export exchange settlement figures, which show exports of sugar in 1950 as valued at $74.3 million and in 1951 at $49.8 million. These latter figures are more in line with the figures for quantities exported, since the Customs figures indicate an apparent doubling of the dollar price of sugar exported. No explanation has been obtainable of this wide discrepancy, though smaller discrepancies might easily arise from differences in methods of calculation.

[b] Not shown separately.

Principal postwar exports from Formosa to the United States were tea, citronella, and hats (of straw, palm, and grass); and the principal imports were artificial fertilizers, soy beans, medicines, condensed milk, raw cotton, electrical machinery, and aircraft (including parts and accessories).

There is general concurrence among postwar American visitors to Formosa in the view that, on the whole, substantial progress has been made there since the Chinese reoccupation.. Those who differentiate between the parts played respectively by the National Government and by the Provincial Government speak more enthusiastically of the latter. Nevertheless, since the National Government has jurisdiction over some of the enterprises and exercises jointly with the Provincial Government jurisdiction over other enterprises that have contributed to economic recovery, the former must share with the latter the credit for what has been accomplished.

General MacArthur's observations, which were based on a short visit to Formosa in August 1950, are quoted below:

> I superficially went through Formosa. I was surprised at the contentment I found there.
>
> I found that the people were enjoying a standard of living which was quite comparable to what it was before the war. I found a financial system which at that time was about as sound as anything in the Far East except Japan. I found representative government being practiced.
>
> In one legislative group I went into, I found of the 21 people there were 19 elected Formosans. I went into their courts. I found a judicial system which I thought was better than a great many of the other countries in Asia.
>
> I went into their schools. I found that their primary instruction was fully on a standard with what was prevalent in the Far East. I was surprised.
>
> I found many things that I could criticize, too, but I believe sincerely that the standard of government that he [Chiang Kai-shek] is setting in Formosa compares favorably with many of the democracies of the world.[8]

A more up-to-date American estimate of the performance of the regime in Formosa is that of Mr. Karl L. Rankin, the American Minister at Taipei, who, while enroute to the United States, gave press correspondents at Hong Kong on May 11, 1952 a written statement. He declared that he was much more optimistic about Formosa than he had been 21 months earlier when he first took up his post. He said that increased United States aid was beginning to show results, and that there were signs of greater free world unity with regard to the Far

[8] *Military Situation in the Far East,* Hearings p. 112.

East, but he attributed his optimism most immediately to the accomplishments of the National Government and the Formosan people. He noted that the budget was now almost in balance, despite the fact that revenues covered barely one half of the expenditures, and he pointed out that production was rising steadily and the strength of the Nationalist defense establishment mounting.[9]

[9] *New York Times* (May 11, 1952).

CHAPTER 7.

Development of United States Policy Regarding Formosa

B EFORE the Second World War, United States concern with Formosa was almost wholly commercial,
and even American commercial interests were relatively
small. Formosa was unique among the areas in the Far
East of comparable accessibility and populousness in
the fact that no American missionary establishments or
other philanthropic and cultural enterprises were
located there. Between 1898 and the outbreak of the
war the United States maintained a consulate at Taipei.

By the time when, fifty years ago, concern for the
preservation of the territorial and administrative integrity of China was first officially and formally declared
to be a feature of United States policy, Formosa had already been ceded to Japan.[1] The United States raised
no questions in regard to the cession when it took place,
nor later in regard to the exercise by Japan of sovereignty over Formosa until after the outbreak of the
Second World War. In brief, not until 1941 did developments in or regarding Formosa pose a problem of
practical political concern to the United States.

With the Chinese reoccupation of Formosa in Septem-

[1] The cession occurred in 1895, whereas it was not until July 3, 1900
that the enunciation of this position was made, in a note addressed by
Secretary of State Hay to the powers.

ber 1945, the island became, *de facto* at least, pending a formalization of its status by a treaty with Japan, a part of the Republic of China, and thus was brought automatically within the scope of the China policy of the United States. To the territory and the people there were then extended the principles, the concerns, the commitments, and the precedents established with respect to China by the historic Far Eastern policy of the United States, except as these had been modified, altered, and subjected to reinterpretation under the stress of war and postwar conditions.

Policy Following the Retreat of the National Government to Formosa

The situation was changed in December 1949 by the withdrawal to Formosa of the National Government with the remnant of its armed forces and substantial holdings in gold. In the United States, an acute public controversy developed as attempts were made to assess blame for the disaster that had overtaken a friendly government which it had been American policy to assist extensively with money, equipment, and good offices. The controversy was not made less bitter by the fact that the American Government had just turned its back on Chiang Kai-shek, despite the fact that Chiang and his supporters were out-and-out anti-Communists.

One section of the American public was disposed to assume that the United States had had it within its power to control the course of events in China. Critics charged that American policies had been shaped by inexperienced and visionary theorists or by Communist sympathizers in the State Department. The American Government itself has contended that the result of the "civil strife" in China could not have been changed by anything that the United States did or could have done within the reasonable limits of its capabilities.

This controversy made it difficult for the United States Government to adjust itself to the new situation or to formulate a course of action that would meet the actual circumstances and satisfy the demands of its critics. The central question, whether to return to a policy of supporting the National Government or to develop some other means of keeping Formosa out of Communist hands, was complicated by another issue—namely, the advisability and practicability of withholding recognition from the Communist regime, which by that time exercised physical control over the greater part of China, in favor of continuing to recognize the National Government which still exercised authority over a small fraction of the national territory. A number of countries, notably Great Britain and India, early made their decision on this matter and recognized the Central People's Government of the Republic of China, and by that or by express action withdrew recognition from the National Government.

In the United States, however, developments in China were interpreted as creating an additional Soviet-Communist threat to the national interest and to national security. Many Americans insisted that the United States should not recognize the Central People's Government and that it should take positive action to prevent Formosa from falling into Communist hands. On January 2, 1950, Senator Knowland made public the text of a letter from former President Hoover advocating this course. The considerations that Mr. Hoover emphasized were the need (1) of having a wall against communism in the Pacific, (2) of securing the defense of Japan and the Philippines, (3) of preventing Chinese diplomatic establishments in the United States from becoming nests of Communist conspiracy, (4) of preventing another Communist member from being seated in the United Nations Security Council, (5) of keeping a Communist China from taking part in the treaty with Japan, (6) of saving southeast Asia from communism by maintaining in Formosa at least a symbol of resistance, and (7) of keeping alive the hope of bringing China back into the path of freedom.[2] The course proposed by Mr. Hoover received prompt support from Senator Taft, who expressed himself in favor of taking steps to see that the Communists should not cross over to Formosa even though it might be necessary to use the United States Navy to ensure this.

The Administration, as was later revealed, did not share these opinions.[3] The conclusions of the Department of State, based on studies instituted by it in the latter part of 1949, were that Formosa could not be held against a determined attack from the mainland without the use of American forces and that the island would probably fall during 1950. Secretary of State Acheson later stated that the estimate of the State Department

[2] *Congressional Record,* daily ed. (Jan. 5, 1950), pp. 86-87.

[3] *Military Situation in the Far East,* Hearings before the Senate Committee on Armed Services and the Committee on Foreign Relations, 82 Cong. 1 sess. (1951), pp. 1667-79.

During the heat of public debate, critics of the Administration obtained a Department of State document entitled "Policy Information Paper—Formosa." This paper had been prepared for the guidance of Information Officers in drafting material for broadcasting and other information media. It contained tentative estimates of probable developments in Formosa, but Administration spokesmen insisted that it did not reflect fixed policy, as the critics maintained. It was later in commenting on this document and on the probable effect of its publication that Secretary Acheson disclosed what had been the considerations underlying the course of the Department of State.

in 1949 had not differed from that of the other inter-
ested departments of the governments, including the
military.[4]

On January 5, 1950 President Truman issued a policy
statement regarding Formosa. He began with a reference
to traditional United States policy toward China and
expressly to the principle of respect for the territorial
integrity of China, which, he pointed out, had been reaffirmed in the United Nations General Assembly resolution of December 8, 1949. That resolution had called
on all states "to refrain from (a) seeking to acquire
spheres of influence or to create foreign controlled regimes within the territory of China; and (b) seeking to
obtain special rights within the territory of China." He
said that these principles had a specific application to
Formosa, which, in keeping with the Cairo and the
Potsdam Declarations, had been turned over to Generalissimo Chiang Kai-shek when Japan surrendered.
He said that the subsequent exercise of Chinese authority in Formosa had been accepted by the United States
and the other allied powers. He then went on to say:

> The United States has no predatory designs on Formosa
> or on any other Chinese territory. The United States has no
> desire to obtain special rights or privileges or to establish
> military bases on Formosa at this time. Nor does it have any
> intention of utilizing its armed forces to interfere in the
> present situation. The United States Government will not
> pursue a course which will lead to involvement in the civil
> conflict in China.
> Similarly, the United States Government will not provide
> military aid or advice to Chinese forces on Formosa. In the
> view of the United States Government, the resources on
> Formosa are adequate to enable them to obtain the items
> which they consider necessary for the defense of the island.
> The United States Government proposes to continue under

[4] The same, p. 1682.

existing legislative authority the present ECA program of economic assistance.

On the same day, the Secretary of State commented on the statement to press correspondents in the form of "extemporaneous remarks." He explained that the President's statement, while containing little that was new, had been prompted by the prevailing confusion abroad arising from the public discussion of the Formosa question in the United States. This discussion, Mr. Acheson said, had aroused a great deal of speculation, which if allowed to continue would be prejudicial to American interests. In answer to a question concerning the fact that the President's disclaimer of an intent to establish military bases in Formosa had been qualified by the phrase "at this time," the Secretary said that it was "a recognition of the fact that in the unlikely and unhappy event that our forces might be attacked in the Far East the United States must be completely free to take whatever action in whatever area is necessary for its own security."[5]

The President's statement was bitterly attacked by the Republican opposition in the Congress. Senator Taft said that the rejection of the idea of using American armed forces to stop the advance of communism in the Far East was inconsistent with what the United States had agreed to do toward stopping the advance of communism in Europe.[6] Senator Vandenberg, in a statement delivered to the press, declared in part:

Every practical discouragement to Communist conquest, short of active American military participation, should be pursued in China and throughout the Far East. . . . The rights of Formosans themselves must be consulted. The permanent status of Formosa must be recognized as dependent

[5] U. S. Department of State, *Bulletin*, Vol. 22 (Jan. 16, 1950), pp. 79-81.
[6] *Congressional Record*, daily ed. (Jan. 5, 1950), p. 93.

upon the ultimate Japanese peace treaty. The vital interest
of the United Nations must be recognized. . . .[7]

Senator Smith of New Jersey proposed that there
should be established pending the final determination
of Formosa's status, "a joint political authority and responsibility there between ourselves, the Nationalists,
and the Formosan people." He favored asking the Nationalists to cease, during such a "friendly and peaceful
occupation, . . . all aggressive action against the Communists from Formosa." He envisioned the adoption of
a policy there "to develop the economy of the island for
the benefit of the population, and to establish firmly the
institutions and practices of democratic self-government." This, he expected, would be accomplished with
United States economic aid, but the United States
would support the National Government "if necessary,
against aggression by outside forces." He thought that
such a course would allow the United States to "pursue
its historic policy of friendship and support for a free
Chinese people without assuming a dangerous and un-
limited military commitment, and . . . would go far to
deter the Communists from an invasion attempt." He
further recommended that "a full report of this action,
if taken, should be made to the United Nations, stating
that our purpose is to maintain the peace until the
ultimate sovereignty of the island can be determined.[8]

On the other hand, the supporters of the Administration in the Congress came to the defense of the announced position. Senator Connally said:

If we should go into Formosa and occupy it, we would
have a liability on our hands instead of an asset. The Chiefs

[7] The same, p. 107.
[8] The same (Jan. 9, 1950), pp. 226, 227.

of Staff have found that Formosa would be of no strategic value to us. We have Japan at the north, then Okinawa, then the Philippines. That is our line of defense to the east of Formosa, and none of those places involve the question of Communist government or Communist attack.[9]

Senator Taft brought up the subject of Formosa again on the Senate floor on January 11. He said that "there is not the slightest evidence that Russia will go to war with us because we interfere with a crossing to Formosa. It is hardly possible to see how the Chinese Communists by themselves can begin a war against the United States, or why they should do so." He conceded that "in recent months it has, of course, been very doubtful whether aid to the National Government could be effective, and no one desires to waste American efforts." But Formosa, he said,

. . . is a place where a small amount of aid and at a very small cost, can prevent the further spread of communism. Such action does not commit us to backing the Nationalist Government in any prolonged war against the Chinese Communists. We can determine later whether we ever wish to recognize the Chinese Communists and what the ultimate disposition of Formosa shall be. . . .

The status of Formosa . . . should certainly be kept free for determination until the peace treaty has been written with Japan. Formosa must be legally a part of Japan, for it is difficult to see how the mere declaration of the President at Cairo or Potsdam can change that status without a treaty. One thing is certain, if the Communists take over Formosa, we will have just as much chance of setting up an independent republic of Formosa as we have of returning the . . . [eastern] German provinces from Poland to Germany. . . .

Those who argue against any action in Formosa are curiously inconsistent. . . . Here is a small area of the world where, with no difficulty or expense, we could prevent the spread of Communism to an island which might be of great

[9] The same, p. 245.

strategic value and whose people desire to be independent.[10]

On January 12 Secretary of State Acheson made an address before the National Press Club in which he outlined the broad considerations on which United States policy in the Far East was then being based. Much of what he said related to the course that had been followed with respect to Formosa. He referred to the fall of the National Government on the mainland despite the "tremendous economic and military support and backing" accorded to Chiang Kai-shek by the United States, and he declared that Chiang had in the course of the four years since the end of the war completely lost the support of his own people. He observed that communism was the spearhead of Soviet Russian imperialism and its aim was to deprive Asian peoples of their national independence, and that the Soviet Union was detaching and absorbing large areas of China. He expressed the belief that the significance of this most important fact would only be obscured if the United States indulged in the folly of ill-conceived adventures and deflected from the Soviet Union the righteous wrath and the hatred of the Chinese people which was bound to develop. He emphasized first, that the United States must take the position, which it had always taken, that "any one who violates the integrity of China is the enemy of China" and second, the need "to keep our own purposes perfectly straight . . . and not get them mixed up with the legal quibbles or [with] the attempt to do one thing and really achieve another."

Mr. Acheson then went on to discuss American security in the Pacific. He defined the defensive perimeter of the United States in those waters as running along the

[10] The same (Jan. 11, 1950), pp. 311, 312.

Aleutians to Japan, thence to the Ryukyus (Okinawa) and the Philippines.[11] These, he declared, "must and will be held." He added that "so far as the military security of other areas in the Pacific is concerned, it must be clear that no person can guarantee these areas against military attack. . . . Should such an attack occur . . . the initial reliance must be on the people attacked to resist it and then upon the commitments of the entire civilized world under the Charter of the United Nations."

The Secretary of State affirmed that the susceptibility of many areas and many countries in the Pacific to subversion could not be disposed of by military means. American assistance can be effective, he said, "when it is the missing component in a situation that might otherwise be solved," but it cannot furnish the determination, the will, and the loyalty of a people to its government. He finally made a reference to charges of inconsistency in the policy of the government as between the course pursued in relation to one country and that pursued in relation to some other country. That charge, he said, was based on the fallacious idea that the United States must always act in the same way in every country of the world, in disregard of the differences in American interests or of those wider interests that affect American interests.[12]

The public discussion of Formosa continued, though with gradually abating intensity. There were further statements of the intentions of the Administration in support of the course that had been announced. These

[11] Mr. Acheson in his testimony before the Senate Armed Services and Foreign Relations Committees on June 2, 1951 explained that within this perimeter United States forces were present "by right"—that is, in Japan, Okinawa, and the Philippines, *Military Situation in the Far East*, Hearings, p. 1816.

[12] U. S. Department of State, *Bulletin*, Vol. 22 (Jan. 23, 1950), pp. 111-18.

were largely repetitive or elaborative of the statement made by Mr. Acheson.

A year later, on June 1, 1951, Secretary of State Acheson testified before the Armed Services Committee and the Foreign Relations Committee of the Senate that United States policy with regard to Formosa during the period from October 1948 to June 25, 1950 had comprised four elements, namely: (1) the United States recognized that Formosa had a strategic importance for the United States; (2) this importance called for keeping Formosa out of the hands of an unfriendly power and not for the occupation or the use of Formosa by the United States; (3) with the existing strength of the United States armed forces at that time it was not possible to commit any forces whatever to the defense of Formosa; and (4) the State Department should do its best by diplomatic and economic means to keep Formosa from falling into hostile hands. He said that in August 1949 he had "reported" that he could no longer guarantee that economic and diplomatic means would succeed in keeping Formosa out of potentially hostile hands.[13] An implication of the Secretary's statement was that in 1949 the Government of the United States did not consider it wise to commit the prestige of this country to an undertaking to keep Formosa out of communist hands at a time when, in its judgment, we did not possess adequate means to make such an undertaking effective.

Policy Following the Outbreak of the Korean Conflict

On June 27, 1950, two days after the North Korean Communist forces attacked the Republic of Korea,

[13] *Military Situation in the Far East,* Hearings, pp. 1671, 1672.

President Truman issued a statement which heralded a significant shift in American policy.

The part of the statement that bore on Formosa reads as follows:

The attack upon Korea makes it plain beyond all doubt that communism has passed beyond the use of subversion to conquer independent nations and will now use armed invasion and war. It has defied the orders of the Security Council of the United Nations issued to preserve international peace and security. In these circumstances the occupation of Formosa by Communist forces would be a direct threat to the security of the Pacific area and to the United States forces performing their lawful and necessary functions in that area.

Accordingly I have ordered the Seventh Fleet to prevent any attack on Formosa. As a corollary of this action I am calling upon the Chinese Government on Formosa to cease all air and sea operations against the mainland. The Seventh Fleet will see that this is done. The determination of the future status of Formosa must await the restoration of security in the Pacific, a peace settlement with Japan, or consideration by the United Nations.[14]

In accordance with the request of the United States Government, the National Government of China ordered its Navy and its Air Force to cease attacks on the Chinese mainland. However, on July 7, the National Government ordered the resumption of operations in connection with the search and seizure of vessels flying either the Chinese Nationalist or the Chinese Communist flags, giving the reason that since its discontinuance, in response to President Truman's request, of operations against the mainland, large quantities of supplies had been passing into Chinese ports which previously had been effectively closed by those operations. It also ordered its Air Force to resume reconnaissance flights, maintaining that it should be allowed to defend

[14] U. S. Department of State, *Bulletin*, Vol. 23 (July 3, 1950), p. 5.

its many island possessions lying between Formosa and the mainland.[15] The United States did not declare what its attitude was on this matter, but on July 16 General MacArthur reiterated that the Seventh Fleet would prevent further Nationalists attacks upon the mainland.

On July 19 President Truman in a message to the Congress on the Korean situation, amplified his statement of June 27.[16] He reaffirmed the disclaimer of United States territorial ambitions or desire to seek special privileges in Formosa. What the United States desired was, he said, that Formosa should not become embroiled in hostilities disturbing to the peace of the Pacific and that all questions regarding Formosa should be settled by peaceful means as envisaged in the Charter of the United Nations. He declared that the existing military neutralization of the island was without prejudice to the solution of the political questions involved.

On July 28 the Department of State announced the assignment to Taipei of a diplomatic representative to the National Government, with the rank of chargé d'affaires.[17] A spokesman of the State Department said that the new appointment did not reflect any change in United States policy toward Formosa. The step taken was nevertheless significant of the greater importance now attached to Formosa and to the maintenance of close contact with the National Government. It also indicated a stiffening of the intention not to recognize the

[15] *New York Times* (July 8, 1950).

[16] U. S. Department of State, *Bulletin,* Vol. 23 (July 31, 1950), pp. 165-66.

[17] After the recall of Ambassador Stuart to Washington for consultation in 1949 the United States diplomatic mission in China had been headed by a chargé d'affaires. The mission had not, however, followed the National Government from the mainland but had remained at Hong Kong. On December 23, 1949 the chargé went to Formosa where he became the diplomatic representative of the United States.

Communist People's Government of the People's Republic of China.

On July 31 General MacArthur arrived in Taipei, where he held conferences with Generalissimo Chiang Kai-shek and other Nationalist leaders. On the following day, General MacArthur said that plans had been made to co-ordinate steps by United States and Chinese forces to meet any attack that a hostile force might launch against the island, and he expressed confidence that such an attack would have little chance of success.[18] The Generalissimo for his part announced that an agreement had been reached on all the problems that had been discussed and that the foundations had been laid for joint defense of Formosa and for Sino-American military co-operation.[19] General MacArthur's return to Japan was followed shortly by the arrival in Tokyo of Mr. Harriman, Special Assistant to President Truman, for the announced purpose of conferring with General MacArthur on the political situation in the Far East.[20] On August 4 General MacArthur's deputy chief of staff, Major General Fox, arrived in Taipei to establish a permanent liaison with the National Government. These visits, occurring so close together, occasioned an expression of concern in London that a change in United States policy with regard to Formosa might be impending. In view of the fact that Great Britain no longer recognized the National Government, the British Government was apprehensive lest, as a consequence of such a change, Britain might be dragged into vigorous joint action by the United States and the National Government of China against the Chinese Communists.[21]

[18] *New York Times* (Aug. 1 ,1950).
[19] The same, (Aug. 2, 1950).
[20] The same, (Aug. 4, 1950).
[21] The same, (Aug. 5, 1950).

The Department of State took occasion to emphasize that General MacArthur's visit to Taipei had related solely to military matters concerning the defense of Formosa.

It is clear that the key factors in the shift that took place in the policy of the United States with respect to its relations with the National Government of China and to the keeping of Formosa out of Communist hands were the state of American public opinion, the outbreak of the conflict in Korea, and the intervention of the Chinese Communist regime in that conflict. The extent of this shift can be measured in various ways. One example will suffice.

Prior to President Truman's announcement in January 1950 of a "hands-off" policy towards Formosa, the Joint Chiefs of Staff had recommended a "different course"—one of extending military aid to the National Government in Formosa.[22] This recommendation was rejected because of a political consideration. This consideration, as stated by the Secretary of State in his Press Club speech of a few days later, was the paramount importance of keeping the record of the United States clear in respect to maintaining the principle of respecting the territorial integrity of China in order that the fact of Soviet expansion would stand out for all to see.

When the Communist attack in Korea gave rise to the conviction that communism had passed from the use of subversion to the use of armed force, the long-range political consideration that had led to the adoption of the "hands-off" policy was outweighed by considerations of the necessity of meeting an immediate military threat. The policy of "neutralizing" the island was decided upon. The intervention of Communist China on the

[22] *Military Situation in the Far East*, Hearings, p. 882.

side of the North Koreans in October 1950 strengthened the American decision that Formosa should not be permitted to fall into Chinese Communist hands. At this point the shipment of arms to the National Government was resumed and a substantial military mission was sent to Formosa.

The development of policy did not rest here. Events in Korea and in the Far East generally, as well as increasing public tension in the United States, urged the American Government on until firm positions began to be taken. The full extent of this development was revealed by the tone and content of an address delivered before the China Institute on May 18, 1951, by Dean Rusk, Assistant Secretary of State for Far Eastern Affairs.[23] The remarks of Mr. Rusk that bore most directly on policy toward Formosa were as follows:

We recognize the National Government of the Republic of China even though the territory under its control is severely restricted. We believe it more authentically represents the views of the great body of the people of China, particularly their historic demand for independence from foreign control. That government will continue to receive important aid and assistance from the United States. Under the circumstances, however, such aid in itself cannot be decisive to the future of China. The decision and the effort are for the Chinese people, pooling their efforts, wherever they are, in behalf of China.

This was taken to be the equivalent of an announcement that the United States was unqualifiedly supporting the National Government of China.

On account of this implication the statement was criticized in some quarters because of the possible adverse effect that might follow in Great Britain and in

[23] U. S. Department of State, *Bulletin,* Vol. 24 (May 28, 1951), pp. 746, 848.

Western Europe. There was, however, no official repudiation of Mr. Rusk's statement. The presumption remained that it reflected a considered official position.

It has been shown how the policy of the United States toward the National Government of China and hence toward Formosa underwent considerable change between the end of 1949 and the end of 1951. We now turn to the subject of the assistance, both economic and military, extended by the United States to the National Government and hence to the island of Formosa during this same period.

United States Economic Aid

Roughly speaking the American aid program falls into three stages. The first stage can be identified as the period during which Formosa was a residuary legatee of the then operating China aid program. The second stage corresponded approximately with the period when public discussion in the United States of American policy in the Far East was most intense. During this period, the continuation and expansion of economic aid served as a partial compensation for a suspension of military aid and for an unwillingness to make drastic policy commitments respecting Formosa. It could also be regarded as a hedge against the possible immediate consequences of failure to adopt a positive course, since it was calculated to enable the National Government to deal with the internal problems of Formosa and to stabilize its position. The third stage, marked by a resumption of military assistance, was prompted by the outbreak of the conflict in Korea.

When in December 1949 the National Government

of China was supplanted on the mainland of China by the Communist regime, Formosa inherited the residue of the China aid program of the United States, the current basis of which was the China Aid Act of 1948. That act had authorized $338 million, which the later appropriation reduced to $275 million, to be applied under the applicable provisions of the Economic Cooperation Act of 1948, together with a further appropriation of $125 million for additional aid to China through grants, on such terms as the President might determine, without reference to the provisions of the Economic Cooperation Act of 1948.[24] This additional appropriation was intended to enable the Chinese government to purchase military supplies and equipment wherever it wished.

Operations of the Economic Cooperation Administration in China were instituted in pursuance of an Economic Aid Agreement concluded between the United States and the Republic of China in July 1948.[25] Under the agreement the United States undertook to furnish China such assistance as might be requested by it and approved by the Government of the United States. The Chinese Government pledged itself to undertake a vigorous program of self-help in order to create more stable conditions in China and to improve commercial relations with other countries. Aid was actually provided through an ECA administrator and through the Joint (Chinese and American) Commission on Rural Reconstruction (JCRR).[26] Even before the transfer of the seat of the National Government to Formosa, that

[24] 62 Stat. 159; 62 Stat. 143 ff.
[25] For text of the Agreement see U. S. Department of State, *United States Relations with China* (August 1949), pp. 994-1001.
[26] See below, pp. 137-39.

province, as an integral part of China, had received a share of this aid.

Substantial ECA operations in Formosa began in January 1949. However, Lorin P. Craig, the first ECA director appointed there, had made, during the previous year while serving as an Economic Analyst assigned to the American Consulate General at Taipei, a comprehensive "pre-project survey" of the island. In Formosa a close working relationship was established with the (Chinese) China-United States Aid Agreement Administration and with the J. G. White Engineering Corporation, a private New York concern that had been engaged by the Chinese Government to give technical advisory service on industrial reconstruction and replacement projects.

ECA also worked closely with the Board of Trustees for Rehabilitation Affairs (BOTRA), a post-UNRRA agency of the United Nations. The principal activities of BOTRA were the supervision of a DDT-producing plant at Kaohsiung, work with the Agricultural Machinery Operations Management Organization, and the supervision of fishing fleets at Keelung and Kaohsiung. Among the Chinese governmental agencies with which ECA has principally dealt are the National Resources Commission, the Taiwan Food Bureau, the Department of Agriculture and Forestry of the Provincial Government, and the Bank of Taiwan.

To promote the effectiveness of the ECA program in co-ordination with Chinese self-help measures there was established a Taiwan Joint Committee on United States Aid (CUSA). The committee included as ex-officio members heads of concerned departments and agencies of the Provincial Government, the regional directors in Formosa of ECA, the project manager of the

J. G. White Engineering Corporation, and a representative of the JCRR. There was provision also for other members to be appointed by the chairman of the Provincial Council, by ECA, and by CUSA. This committee, though wholly advisory, came to play an important part in economic planning for Formosa.

In 1949 the ECA program for Formosa had been almost wholly confined to the distribution of commodities, chiefly medical supplies and yarns, which had been transferred from the mainland in anticipation of the Communist take-over there; and of fertilizers that had been imported by ECA and distributed to farmers under the supervision of the JCRR. The J. G. White Engineering Corporation, for its part, gave technical assistance principally in the fields of power, transportation, communications, general industries, and forestry.

Programs for the following years were drawn up on a larger scale. Their scope is shown by the following table giving the aggregate estimates (in thousands of United States dollars) for the fiscal years 1950 and 1951 by types of assistance.

	Fiscal Year	
	1950 (3rd and 4th quarters)	1951
A. Commodity Program	7,227	25,984
B. Industrial Maintenance and Replacement ..	910	9,791
C. Technical Assistance Program	–	690
D. Joint Committee for Rural Reconstruction .	–	300
Total	8,137	36,765[27]

As regards the program for the fiscal year 1950, estimated sales proceeds from supplied commodities and services to be applied in addition to appropriated funds were $1,380,000 for the commodity program and

[27] Economic Cooperation Administration, *Program Operation Report: Mission to China* (Nov. 10, 1950), pp. 4-5.

$2,225,000 for the Industrial Maintenance and Replacement Program. For the 1950 program, because of the uncertain military and political situation in the early part of the year, two principles were adopted: (1) commodities were scheduled on a "pipe-line" basis (devised to meet immediate requirements without stockpiling); and (2) industrial projects were to be of short-range types designed to produce early benefits, the types selected being for the most part related to maintenance and replacement of essential industrial equipment. After June 1950, in response to the changes in the Far East brought about by the implications of the Korean conflict, longer-term projects were approved and initiated.[28] By the end of December 1950, against a total of appropriated funds amounting to $40 million, $35 million had been obligated, leaving an unobligated balance of $5 million; and aid of all types extended to Formosa from funds appropriated since the inception of the China Aid Program totaled $62.8 million.

Prior to June 1950, procurement for Formosa under ECA financing was handled largely by United States Government agencies. Thereafter, although a substantial portion of procurement was opened to competitive bidding by private concerns, orders for the most part were placed through Chinese governmental purchasing agencies. These practices have been criticized by American businessmen as likely to discourage the development of free enterprise in Formosa, both American and Chinese, in the field of foreign trade, especially since ECA is supplying nearly all of Formosa's import exchange requirements. It is understood, however, that ECA has recently been considering a change of policy

[28] Economic Cooperation Administration, *Tenth Annual Report to Congress for the Quarter ended September 30, 1950*, p. 79.

in favor of an increased volume of procurement through private commercial channels.

Early in 1951 it was decided, in view of the heavy drain in the previous year on Formosan gold and foreign exchange reserves, to make an additional allocation of $16 million in ECA funds for assistance in Formosa. Later in June supplemental aid of $41.7 million was provided by the transfer of funds for inclusion in the allocations for Formosa prior to the end of the fiscal year. The total program from June 1, 1950 to June 30, 1951 amounted to $98 million.[29]

In pursuance of the Mutual Security Act (Public Law 165, 82 Cong., 1 Sess.) which was approved on October 10, 1951, the Economic Cooperation Administration was superseded by the Mutual Security Agency, under which economic aid to Formosa has continued.

The China Aid Act of 1948 provided that funds up to 10 per cent of the amount appropriated for economic aid to China—which amount was $275 million—or its equivalent in local currency derived from the sale of ECA commodities could be used to finance a rural reconstruction program. The act provided that the President of China should appoint three members and the President of the United States two members to a Commission which should "formulate and carry out a program for reconstruction in rural areas of China. . . ." An exchange of notes between the Chinese and the United States governments on August 4, 1948, formalized the establishment of a Joint Commission on Rural Reconstruction.

[29] The material for the foregoing section has been drawn mostly from the Economic Cooperation Administration, *Thirteenth Report to Congress for the Quarter ended June 30, 1951* and previous reports; *Program Operations Report: Mission to China* (Nov. 10, 1950); and *U.S. Economic Assistance to Formosa, 1 January to 31 December, 1950.*

The Commission was for practical purposes an organization allied with ECA. Its head offices had been in Canton but were transferred to Taipei when the southern advance of the Chinese Communist armies began. When the ECA headquarters in China was also transferred to Formosa, Raymond T. Moyer, a member of the JCRR, was appointed chief ECA representative and held both positions concurrently.

The JCRR from the outset of its operations in Formosa attacked the problem of agrarian reform. In Formosa more than half a million agricultural families were trying to make a living on 2 million acres of tilled land. About one third of the farmers were owners; 27 per cent part owners and part tenants; and 40 per cent wholly tenants. In the past, land rents were generally much higher than the productivity of the soil warranted; they amounted normally to somewhere between 55 per cent and 60 per cent of the crop. With the inclusion of the cost of fertilizer, seed, equipment, and buildings, there was little possibility that a tenant could save enough to become an owner, no matter how hard he worked or how frugally he lived. Then too, tenants were subject to insecurity of tenure, because of the practice of canceling leases without due compensation when a higher rental was offered. As a result of these conditions the peasant population suffered from disease and undernourishment, which led to rural instability and provided a breeding ground for social unrest and discontent.

As a result of the efforts of the JCRR, the Formosan Provincial Government, with the approval of the National Government, initiated a program to cut rentals to 37.5 per cent of the main crop and to give tenants a greater security of tenure. All lease contracts had to

be registered with the authorities, new contracts had to
be written for a period of from 3 to 6 years and could
not be terminated within that period, and existing contracts had to be revised to conform to the new system.
The JCRR assistance consisted in providing funds for
the execution of this program. As a next step, the JCRR
co-operated with the Chinese Research Institute of Land
Economics in a project for analyzing the effects of farm
rent reduction upon the rural economy, with a view to
determining what changes in the program might be
needed. In 1949 the JCRR accorded financial and technical assistance to the Provincial Government of Formosa in undertaking a complete reorganization of the
farmers' associations, which had disintegrated after the
Japanese surrender, and to effect an amalgamation between them and the rural co-operatives.

Military Aid

In January 1950 President Truman announced that
the United States would provide no further military aid
or advice to the National Government of China. Prior
to this announcement, however, military equipment had
gone to Formosa under the $125 million military aid
program provided for by the China Aid Act of 1948.
This action was taken at the request of the National
Government. More than half of the shipments made
under the program were thus consigned. In addition,
the Chinese Government itself transferred to Formosa
considerable quantities of supplies and equipment previously acquired from the United States at a fraction of
the procurement costs. During 1949 shipments to Formosa had included 123,000 .30 caliber rifles, 68 million
rounds of .38 caliber ammunition, 19 million rounds

of .45 caliber ammunition, 30 Sherman tanks from the
United Kingdom, 100 light tanks, 100 scout cars, and
200 AR 6 aircraft.[30] Finally, provision for the continuation of such aid was made in the Mutual Defense Assistance Act of 1949, as follows:

> Sec. 303. In consideration of the concern of the United
> States in the present situation in China, there is hereby
> authorized to be appropriated to the President, out of any
> moneys in the Treasury not otherwise appropriated, the
> sum of $75,000,000 in addition to funds otherwise provided
> as an emergency fund for the President, which may be ex-
> pended to accomplish in that general area the policies and
> purposes declared in this Act. Certification by the President
> of the amounts expended out of funds authorized here-
> under, and that it is unadvisable to specify the nature of
> such expenditures, shall be a sufficient voucher for the
> sums expended.[31]

Action under this authority was suspended after the
President's announcement and remained so until the
outbreak of the Korean war.

At this juncture, the National Government of China
offered, in response to the United Nations resolution
calling for assistance to the Republic of Korea, the services of 33,000 Chinese troops. That offer was not accepted, because, among other reasons, the Joint Chiefs
of Staff believed that whatever might be the military
value of these forces they could function more effectively
in the defense of Formosa than elsewhere.[32]

The security of Formosa had now assumed a new
significance. In July 1950 the Joint Chiefs, in response
to a request from the State Department for views on
Formosa, affirmed that the island was of strategic value
and that the continuation of Chinese Nationalist re-

[30] *Military Situation in the Far East,* Hearings, p. 1930.
[31] 63 stat. 716.
[32] *Military Situation in the Far East,* Hearings, p. 902.

sistance to the Communists was important to the United States. They recommended a policy of protecting Formosa against the Communists, a revival of military aid, and the making of a survey of the Nationalist forces on Formosa by General MacArthur and his staff.[33]

The recommendations of the Joint Chiefs having been approved by the Department of State, the proposed survey was made in August by a mission headed by Major General Fox, Deputy Chief of Staff to General MacArthur. The mission's report was used to develop programs for military assistance to the Nationalists. Since in the summer and autumn of 1950 there were reports of preparations by Chinese Communist forces in south China for amphibious operations, indicating the actuality of a threat of an early action against Formosa, initiation of shipments to Formosa of critically needed ammunition was approved by the Joint Chiefs.[34]

In November and again in December, General MacArthur recommended the use of Chinese Nationalist forces from Formosa as reinforcements in Korea. While this recommendation was not accepted in Washington, the Joint Chiefs reached a tentative agreement in January 1951, on a course of action that might be taken in the event that the United Nations forces were driven out of Korea.[35] This plan provided for the use of the Nationalist forces in operations against the mainland of China, if feasible, but not in Korea. Later in the same month, a supplementary program for the Army military assistance for Formosa was approved, and in late February, Air and Navy programs were approved. In March the Joint Chiefs recommended and the government ap-

[33] The same, p. 903.
[34] The same.
[35] The same.

proved the establishment of a military assistance advisory group and training mission for Formosa. The Joint Chiefs studied and recommended a program of military aid calling for an expenditure of some $300 million for the National Government on Formosa to be provided in due course.[36] The Mutual Defense Assistance program through 1952 provides for supplying about 70 per cent of the equipment recommended in the report of the Fox survey group.

On April 20 announcement was made by the Department of Defense that there was being sent to the National Government on Formosa a military assistance advisory group, comprising 116 officers and men, to be headed by Major General William C. Chase. It was stated that the advisory group would operate as a part of the United States Embassy at Taipei and would perform the usual duties connected with the furnishing of military assistance by the United States to foreign governments. Later it was disclosed that the advisory group would be supplemented by the addition of another 400 to 500 military instructors and advisers.[37] The Secretary of State affirmed at a press conference on April 25[38] that the assistance to Formosa represented "no change" in policy toward the National Government of China or the Far East in general. He gave a reminder of the fact that United States policy called for the "neutralization" of Formosa, and that the United States Seventh Fleet had been ordered to carry out that policy.

Concurrently, the Department of State released the

[36] The same, pp. 902, 903.
[37] *New York Times* (Apr. 21, 1951); *New York Herald Tribune* (Apr. 24, 1951).
[38] The same (Apr. 26, 1951).

texts of an exchange of notes between the American and the Chinese governments that had taken place earlier, on January 30, regarding the extension of military aid. The exchange of notes provided that the material furnished by the United States would be used by the Chinese Government to maintain its internal security or its legitimate self-defense, and that the Chinese Government would not transfer or use the material for purposes other than those specified without first obtaining the assurances of the United States that such material was not required for other United States purposes. These provisions ruled out the use of the material for an attack on the mainland. There was also provision concerning the status and the facilities to be accorded by the Chinese Government to the personnel assigned by the United States to Formosa for the purpose of furthering the military aid program.[39]

The United States military assistance advisory group entered upon its duties in Formosa in the spring of 1951. In May General Bradley expressed the view that the more the United States strengthens Formosa, the greater will be the confidence developed there and the better will the Chinese there be able to improve the mobility of their reserves. He also expressed the opinion that the concentration of Chinese Communist troops opposite Formosa at that moment was not so formidable as it had been a year earlier. This, he explained, did not mean that they could not invade the island but to do so successfully they would have to build up their forces considerably.[40] Since many of the ships of the Nationalist Navy were inoperable because of a lack of ammunition

---

[39] U. S. Department of State, *Bulletin*, Vol. 24 (May 7, 1951), p. 747.

[40] *Military Situation in the Far East*, Hearings, p. 1078.

and a need for spare parts and repairs, the United States
Navy developed a program to remedy these defects, in
the expectation that within a few months after the program was implemented the condition of the Chinese
naval forces would be greatly improved.[41]

In pursuance of the Mutual Security Act of 1951, referred to earlier in this chapter, the Mutual Defense Assistance Program is now under the supervision and general direction of the Director for Mutual Security. In
a report issued in February 1952, the progress made by
the Military Assistance Advisory group during the first
six months of its functioning on Formosa was described,
in part, as follows:

> . . . activities have centered primarily on reorganization
> of the Chinese military forces and assisting these forces to
> make the best use of their present equipment and supplies.
> In their effort to accomplish this objective, the members
> of the Military Assistance Advisory Group and their col-
> leagues in the Chinese military establishment have made
> intensive inspections and orientation trips to all parts of
> Formosa. These inspections formed the basis for recommen-
> dations subsequently submitted through Chinese channels
> for the reorganization of the Chinese National Government
> forces; for the establishment of training centers, maneuver
> areas, and supply; for maintenance equipment procedures.
> The suggestions made by the United States advisory team
> were readily accepted and partially implemented during the
> period of this survey.
> Progress in Formosa under the MDAP is not readily
> measured in terms of concrete or material accomplishments
> . . . the amount of actual military equipment received dur-
> ing that time [May to October 1951] was relatively small. . . .
> Higher morale and a growing belief in a better future
> are already evident in both the military and civilian popu-
> lations of Formosa. . . . Further progress may be expected
> as the flow of United States aid increases on the basis of
> preparations which are being made at an increasingly rapid

---

[41] The same, p. 1525.

rate by the Chinese military establishment under the guidance of the United States Military Assistance Advisory Group.[42]

According to a press dispatch, under a Taipei May 1, 1952 dateline, the advisory group personnel in Formosa then totaled 400, composed in about equal numbers of officers and enlisted men and that, according to General Chase, that number would be doubled and thus reach its full projected strength within three months. General Chase was quoted as expressing the view that the combat efficiency, morale, and physical condition of the Nationalist army had improved considerably during the past year.[43]

The American economic assistance that was given to Formosa during the period between January and June 1950 when President Truman's policy of withholding military aid from the Nationalist forces on Formosa was in force was undoubtedly of considerable value to the National Government. That assistance, consisting largely of the supplying of medicines, yarns, and fertilizers, helped to ease the problems of the National Government of caring for the heavy influx of Chinese refugees from the mainland and of restoring agricultural production. It is doubtful, however, whether this aid was a material factor in the immunity of the National Government from attack by the Chinese Communists during that period or in the progress achieved toward the political and economic stabilization of Formosa generally. Even if by the end of that period the Communists had completed their preparations for an assault on the island—and the available evidence is that they had not—

[42] U. S. Department of State, *Building a Mutual Defense* (February 1952).

[43] *New York Times* (May 2, 1952).

the season of the year was unpropitious for an amphibious attack. The six months' respite which was given the National Government afforded it an opportunity to make further progress, already begun, toward political reorganization and economic rehabilitation.

CHAPTER 8.

Formosa, the United Nations, and the Japanese Peace Treaty

THE CENTRAL question posed internationally in regard to Formosa, namely that of its political status, arises from the fact that the island is the focal point of a conflict between two rival claimants—the National Government of China and the Central People's Government of the People's Republic—for supreme authority over all of China. Normally a dispute of this character would be essentially an internal Chinese matter. However, one of the rival claimants has openly acknowledged the leadership of the Soviet Union, whose policies have been directed to expanding Soviet influence and domination and whose power threatens the peace and security of other nations. Concern lest loss of the island to the Communist claimant might give Soviet-Communism a material advantage in the world-wide struggle has influenced the attitude and actions of some of the nations that are opposing Communism, most notably those of the United States. At the same time, the other claimant still holds Formosa, an integral part of the national domain; and, equally important, that claimant represents China on the international stage, by sitting as one of the permanent members of the Security Council of the United Nations and by occupying China's seats in the General Assembly and in other organs.

In addition to this central question, others arise which, although peripheral, are none the less important. Among these is that which arises from the fact that the Communist regime in China has shown itself intent upon and able to develop a policy of aggressive expansion, while the National Government, which had never shown such a disposition, is now manifestly incapable of developing such a policy. To states with territorial interests in the Far East (notably Great Britain and France), to states that have security interests in the Far East (especially the United States), and to newly-formed Asian nations, this contrast was and is significant.

To some states these circumstances have suggested the necessity of opposing Communist China, firmly and absolutely and at all points, and thus, by implication, of supporting the National Government and maintaining Formosa as its base. To other states it has suggested the desirability of entering into relations with a regime that exercises *de facto* control over practically the whole territory of China, and thus, actually or by implication, of withdrawing recognition or support from the National Government. In still other cases, intermediate and frequently ambiguous positions have been developed, only to be modified later in the light of changes in the situations. The range of conclusions has been in itself a measure of the extent to which Formosa, from the moment when it became the only area in which the National Government of China really exercised jurisdiction, also became an international problem.

Formosa and the United Nations

Up to the time when the National Government of China retreated from the mainland to Formosa, only

the Soviet Union and some of its satellites had accorded
recognition to the Central People's Government of the
People's Republic of China. By mid-January 1950, however, five members of the United Nations Security
Council (the Soviet Union, Yugoslavia, India, Great
Britain, and Norway) had withdrawn their support from
the National Government and had recognized the Central People's Government. The British *de jure* recognition of the latter on January 6, was an especially severe
blow to the National Government. In all, seventeen out
of sixty members of the United Nations have recognized
the Chinese Communist regime, and among non-mem-
ber nations that are not Soviet satellites Switzerland is
the only one that has recognized that regime. Governments that still recognize the National Government
include, in addition to the United States, all of the
American republics, Belgium, France, and all of the
English-speaking Commonwealth nations other than the
United Kingdom.

The Soviet Government began early to exert pressure
to expel the Nationalist delegates from their seats in the
United Nations and to seat delegates of the Chinese
Communist regime in their places. On December 29,
1949 the Soviet representative in the Security Council
announced his government's support of the contention
of the Chinese Communist regime that the Nationalist
delegation was not qualified to speak for China or the
Chinese people. He did not, however, at that time move
formally to unseat the Nationalist delegation. Later, in
January 1950, he introduced a resolution to that end.[1]
Upon the refusal of the Security Council to put the resolution to an immediate vote, he staged the first of a long

[1] *New York Times* (Jan. 11, 1950).

series of Soviet and satellite "walkouts" from organs of
the United Nations.

Earlier, in September 1949, the Chinese delegation
had placed before the General Assembly a charge of
"threats to the political independence and territorial integrity of China and to the peace of the Far East, resulting from Soviet violations of the Sino-Soviet Treaty of
Friendship and Alliance of 14 August 1945 and from
Soviet violations of the Charter of the United Nations."[2]
Two months later, the charges were considered by the
General Assembly, but no action was taken at that time.
On February 7, 1950 the Chinese delegate presented to
the "Little Assembly," for later submission to the General Assembly, a similar draft resolution. It was not until
two years later that any action was taken. On February
1, 1952 the General Assembly adopted a resolution in
which it was determined "that the Union of Soviet Socialist Republics, in its relations with China since the
surrender of Japan, has failed to carry out the Treaty of
Friendship and Alliance between China and the Union
of Soviet Socialist Republics of 14 August 1945."[3] All this
of course had but an indirect bearing upon Formosa.

While on the one hand the National Government was
striving to maintain its position, and on the other hand
the Soviet Union was making efforts to expel the Nationalist delegation from the United Nations, international opinion fluctuated and was still uncrystallized
when the North Korean Communists attacked the Republic of Korea in June 1950. The initial action of the
Security Council, taken in the absence of the Soviet

[2] U.N. General Assembly, *Plenary Meetings of the General Assembly*,
Agenda Item 68, U.N. Doc. A/1215 (Dec. 6, 1949), pp. 234-36.
[3] U.N. General Assembly, *Resolutions Adopted by the General Assembly during its Sixth Session, 6 November 1951 to 5 February
1952*, Resolution 505, Supplement 20, U.N. Doc. A/2119, p. 4.

representative, committed the United Nations to a course of resisting Communist aggression in Korea. The individual members of the United Nations, other than the states of the Soviet bloc, felt bound by the action of the Security Council. Consequently, on the question of Korea, an issue was created on which the free nations and the countries of the Soviet orbit were ranged on opposite sides. With regard to Formosa, however, the decision made independently by the United States to "neutralize" the island was not generally approved by other members of the United Nations. Later, in October, when the Chinese Communists came to the aid of the North Koreans, the issues of Formosa and of the status of the National Government became more closely linked with those of the Korean problem. Yet, even before that, in August, the Soviet representative, when he had resumed his seat on the Security Council and was its president for that month, had made it quite clear that in the view of the Soviet Government and of the Chinese Communist regime these questions were closely associated with each other. His first action had been to propose an agenda in which consideration of the recognition of the Central People's Government of the People's Republic of China as the only government representing China would precede consideration of the question of Korea.

On August 24, 1950 Foreign Minister Chou En-lai of the Central People's Government in communications to the Secretary-General of the United Nations and to the then president of the Security Council (Malik) revived the question of Formosa. Chou asserted that the United States had moved its Seventh Fleet toward the Straits of Formosa, and he alleged that the United States had landed contingents of its Air Force on the island. He

charged that there had thus been a "direct armed aggression" against Chinese territory and a violation of
the United Nations Charter. The people of China, he
declared, found this action intolerable and were determined to "liberate Taiwan" and other Chinese territory from "the tentacles of United States aggression."
He called upon the Security Council to condemn the
United States for its "criminal" action and to take immediate steps to bring about the withdrawal "of all the
United States armed invading forces from Taiwan and
from other territories belonging to China."[4]

The Department of State promptly announced that
the United States would welcome an examination of
the Formosa problem. It recalled the fact that when the
United States took action to neutralize Formosa it had
at once notified the Security Council and had indicated
that the problem was one that might be considered by
the United Nations.[5] At the instance of a member of the
United States delegation, a letter addressed on August
25 to the Secretary-General by United States Representative Austin was read into the record. The letter contained a denial that the United States had "encroached
on the territory of China" or had taken aggressive action
against China. It stated among other things that the
action of the United States with regard to Formosa had
been one of impartial neutralization taken at a time
when the island was "the scene of conflict with the mainland that threatened the security of United Nations
forces operating in Korea." This action, it declared, was
designed to keep the peace, in full accord with the

---

[4] *United Nations Bulletin* (Sept. 15, 1950), Vol. 9, p. 253; United Nations Security Council, Doc. S/1715 (Aug. 24, 1950).
[5] U. S. Department of State, *Bulletin*, Vol. 23 (Sept. 4, 1950).

spirit of the United Nations Charter, and was without prejudice to the future status of the island. The letter also noted that "with peace re-established, even the most complex political questions are susceptible of solution. In the presence of . . . unprovoked aggression, however, some of these questions may have to be held in abeyance in the interest of the essential security of all."[6]

At the very juncture when the Formosa issue was thus being renewed in the Security Council, General Mac-Arthur sent a message on the subject of Formosa to be read at the 51st encampment of the Veterans of Foreign Wars. That message contained an exposition of the General's views on the strategic importance of the island. In the possession of a hostile power, Formosa would be, he said, "an unsinkable air-craft carrier and submarine tender ideally located to accomplish offensive strategy and at the same time checkmate defensive or counter-offensive operations by friendly forces based on Okinawa and the Philippines." While in other circumstances the letter might have been taken as the expression of a purely military view, the position of its author and its publication at this particular juncture made it suscepti-ble to far broader interpretation.

President Truman, having been advised in advance of the contents of the message, directed that it be with-drawn. General MacArthur complied, but the action came too late to prevent publication by one newspaper that had received an advance copy. It was reproduced in other papers and in the *Congressional Record* of Au-gust 28.

When the Security Council met on August 29, the Soviet representative speaking as president of the Coun-

[6] The same (Sept. 11, 1950), p. 412.

cil presented a provisional agenda that included a new item entitled "Statement of the Central People's Government of the People's Republic of China concerning armed invasion of the territory of China by the Government of the United States of America and Concerning Violation of the Charter of the United Nations." United States representative Austin stated that if Malik would substitute for phraseology in the item the wording "Complaint Regarding Formosa," the United States would be glad to vote in favor of the proposed agenda. President Malik contended that the problem "did not concern Formosa or a complaint about Formosa" but related to the United States invasion of Chinese territory for the purpose of taking it over, contrary to international decisions under which the island had been turned over to China. He contended that if the Council were to state the item differently on the agenda it would be concealing the substance of the matter laid before it. His contention failed to get acceptance by the Council.

Malik, speaking as Soviet representative, then asked, as a matter for exceptional treatment before proceeding to the Korean question, that a decision be taken on the proposal that representatives of the Central People's Government be present for the consideration of the Formosan matter. Despite the objection of the United States to having the item given a priority over the Korean question, President Malik ruled that Soviet representative Malik's request be voted on. The ruling stood in the absence of the required number of votes to defeat it; but the proposal itself, when voted upon, was rejected. Nevertheless, it was later, on September 29, adopted in a modified form. The Council also decided to invite Chinese Communist representatives to be present at its consideration of a Chinese Communist complaint alleging United States bombing of Manchuria.[7]

From the outset, the principal representative of the National Government, Tingfu F. Tsiang, had strongly opposed the inclusion of the subject of Formosa in the agenda of the Security Council. He had emphatically denied that there had been any United States aggression in Formosa, and he objected to the proposal on the grounds that the charge lacked a *prima facie* case; that his Government was in effective control and administration of Taiwan; and that it had legal title to the island. In conclusion, he introduced a resolution to have the Formosa question dropped from the agenda, but this was defeated, as was his later proposal to have the question put before the International Court of Justice.[8]

On September 19 Secretary of State Acheson brought up the question of Formosa in his address at the opening plenary session of the General Assembly. On that occasion, he expressed the belief that the international community had a legitimate interest and concern in having the matter settled by peaceful means.[9] Subsequently, in a letter to the Secretary-General of the United Nations, Mr. Acheson asked that the question of Formosa be added to the agenda as a matter of special and urgent importance.[10] The proposal was adopted by the General

[7] United Nations Security Council, Doc. S/PV. 506 (Sept. 29, 1950), pp. 3-5, text of resolution and record of voting.

[8] United Nations Security Council, Doc. S/PV. 506 (Sept. 26, 1950) p. 22; for full text of debate on "Complaint of Armed Invasion of Taiwan (Formosa)" see U.N. Security Council Doc. S/PV. 482 (Aug. 29, 1950), S/PV. 493 (Aug. 31, 1950), S/PV. 503 p. 29ff. (Sept. 26 1950), S/PV. 504 (Sept. 27, 1950), S/PV. 505 (Sept. 28, 1950), S/PV. 506 (Sept. 29, 1950), S/PV. 507 (Sept. 29, 1950).

[9] U. S. Department of State, *Bulletin,* Vol. 23 (Oct. 2, 1950), p. 526.

[10] The same (Oct. 16, 1950), pp. 607-08.

Assembly on October 7 by a large majority, despite the objections of the Chinese representative, and, for different reasons, of the Soviet Union.

The Chinese representative had observed that it was unprecedented for one member government to call into question the territorial possessions of another and that, in view of the provisions of the United Nations Charter, of the Cairo Declaration, and of the Potsdam Proclamation, it was outside the competence of the General Assembly to discuss the question of Formosa.

The Soviet representative had argued that the inclusion of the item on Formosa in the agenda was contrary to the Charter since the disposition of the island had been earlier determined by international agreements. He had charged that the United States was not questioning these agreements and was preventing the "liberating" of Formosa in order that it might itself establish bases there.

The action of the General Assembly prompted the Chinese Communist Foreign Minister, Chou En-lai, to send a protest to the president of the General Assembly. He declared that in connection with "Taiwan" there existed only the fact of United States aggression there; and so far as the present or future status of "Taiwan" was concerned there was no such thing as the "Question of Formosa."[11]

When the Political and Security Committee of the General Assembly met on November 15 to take up the question of Formosa, the substantial armed intervention of Communist China in Korea on the side of the North Koreans had just occurred. Accordingly, United States Representative Dulles asked to have consideration

[11] United Nations General Assembly, Doc. A/PV. 284 (Sept. 26, 1950), pp. 106-09, text of debate and vote.

of the item on Formosa deferred. The Soviet representative professed to regard Dulles' plea as a desire to postpone committee discussion of the subject until the arrival of the Chinese Communist delegation to take part in the consideration by the Security Council of the Chinese Communist charge of United States aggression in Korea.

Dulles denied that he had meant any such thing. He explained that what he had said was that, in the light of the actions of the Chinese Communist regime, there was a risk that the entire Far East might become engulfed in a war of aggression; that if this occurred a discussion of the long-range future of Formosa would prove to have been somewhat academic; that it was the primary duty of the Security Council to leave no stone unturned to avert disaster; and that the only reason he had suggested postponement of the discussion was that, if held, it might lead to things being said which would complicate the task of the Security Council. The committee then decided to defer the discussion of Formosa until it had dealt with all other pending items.[12]

On November 24 a delegation from the Central People's Government arrived in New York. The provisional agenda for the Security Council, proposed by Yugoslav Representative Bebler, president of the Council for November, contained only one item, comprising two parts: "(A) Complaint of Armed Invasion of Taiwan (Formosa), and (B) Complaint of Aggression against the Republic of Korea." The Council met on November 28.[13] United States Representative Austin, in refuting the Chinese Communist charges of United States aggression

[12] United Nations General Assembly, Doc. A/C 1/SR. 399 (Nov. 15, 1950).
[13] United Nations Press Release SC/1255 (Nov. 27, 1950).

in Formosa, reiterated the position of the United States as it had been set forth by the Secretary of State and other spokesmen. He asked the Chinese Communist representative to state the intentions of the Central People's Government toward Formosa, in particular whether that regime would pledge itself to accept a peaceful settlement of the question or whether it intended to risk the grave disturbance of international peace and security by some warlike act.

Wu Hsiu-chuan, the chief Chinese Communist representative, replied at length in an intemperate vein. He demanded the ousting of the Chinese Nationalist representative from the Security Council and warned that his government would not recognize any action by the Security Council, especially as regards Asia, as long as the "Kuomintang reactionary remnant clique" held the Chinese seat in the United Nations. In regard specifically to Formosa, Wu declared that, regardless of any military measures of obstruction by the United States, and no matter how the United States might arrogate for its purposes the name of the United Nations, the Chinese people were firmly determined to recover from the grip of the American aggressors Taiwan and all other territories belonging to China.

The representative of Nationalist China observed that until he had heard the statement of the Chinese Communist representative he had not thought it possible that any Chinese, even a Communist, would have allowed himself to be led around by his nose to do the bidding of his (Soviet) master. He noted that the statesmen at Cairo and at Potsdam had in fact agreed to restore Formosa to China but with the idea that the island would be developed for the benefit of the Chinese people. It had not been the purpose of these statesmen, Tsiang affirmed, to give Formosa to a puppet regime in China so that the island might be handed over to that regime's overlord in Moscow.

Mr. Austin, on the following day, called on the council to lay aside for the present the fantastic charge of United States aggression against Formosa so that consideration might be given to the serious situation in Korea. On November 30 the Council decisively rejected a Soviet proposal that the United States "immediately withdraw all its air, sea and land forces from the island of Taiwan and from other territories belonging to China." It also rejected a draft Chinese Communist resolution sponsored by the Soviet Union, which would have, among other things, condemned the United States for "its criminal acts of armed aggression" against Chinese territory, including Formosa.[14]

The only further United Nations discussion of the subject of Formosa occurred in the Political and Security Committee of the General Assembly on February 7, 1951, when that body reached this item as the last of its agenda. Both the British and the American representatives expressed themselves in favor of a further deferment of the matter. Mr. Austin observed that when the item was placed on the agenda there had been some hope of settlement, but that the "massive intervention" of Communist China in Korea and the naming by the General Assembly of the Peking Government as an aggressor had changed the situation. The committee adopted British Delegate Jebb's motion for a postponement of discussion of the subject to a future date.[15]

It will be realized that consideration of the problem

[14] United Nations Security Council Doc. S/1921 (Nov. 30, 1950), Complaint of Armed Invasion of Taiwan (Formosa).

[15] United Nations General Assembly, Doc. A/C.1. SR. 442 (Feb. 7, 1951).

of Formosa was only being deferred. The problem had not been resolved. The main elements of the problem, however, were clearly established and can be summarized here for future reference. Foremost is the question which of two Chinese regimes is to be accepted internationally as acting for China. This question is complicated. On the one hand, one of the contenders is a declared aggressor in the Korean conflict and cannot be presumed, therefore, to be willing to accept and to carry out accepted international obligations. On the other hand, the other of the contenders is capable of exercising its authority over only a small part of Chinese territory, a condition of affairs that is unlikely to change unless other and major powers resort to force to overthrow the Communist regime.

Another, and closely related, question was the international status of Formosa. Pending the resolving of the first question, the status of Formosa provided ample occasion for contention. The making of a decision on the first question, however, would simplify a settlement of the second. As matters now stand, both questions are involved with a third question—that of resolving the conflicting views of a number of great and small states, either of Asia or possessing traditional interests in the Far East, on how best those interests might be served.

These basic questions arose and were debated not only in direct connection with Formosa but also simultaneously in connection with the eagerness of the United States to proceed to a peace settlement with Japan.

Formosa and the Japanese Peace Settlement

In October 1950 the Department of State circulated among the governments represented on the Far Eastern

Commission—that is, the thirteen nations which had been most closely concerned on the allied side with the war in the Pacific—a preliminary statement of American suggestions for a proposed Japanese peace treaty. With regard to disposal of Formosa and the Pescadores, it was suggested in this statement that Japan should be required to accept a future decision by the United Kingdom, the Soviet Union, China, and the United States; but that if no decision was reached within a year after the treaty came into effect, the United Nations General Assembly should decide.[16] To this suggestion the Soviet Government replied that the question of returning Formosa and the Pescadores had been decided by the Cairo Declaration and the Potsdam Agreement, and that there was no occasion for a new decision by the four great powers.[17] The United States Government pointed out that, in its opinion, the Cairo Declaration, like other wartime declarations, was "subject to any final peace settlement where all relevant factors should be considered," including the views of the powers not represented at Cairo, as well as the bearing of the United Nations Charter, the obligations of which prevail over any other international agreement.[18]

In a subsequent communication on May 7, 1951, the Soviet Government, commenting on the draft of a peace treaty for Japan which the United States had presented to the concerned allied powers, contended that the draft did not faithfully reflect the surrender terms because it did not provide that "the island of Taiwan [Formosa] and the Pescadores should be returned to China."[19] The

---

[16] U. S. Department of State, *Bulletin,* Vol. 23 (Dec. 4, 1950), p. 881.
[17] The same, pp. 881-82.
[18] U. S. Department of State, *Bulletin,* Vol. 24 (Jan. 8, 1951), pp. 65-66.
[19] The same (May 28, 1951), p. 857.

United States Government replied on this point, as follows:

> The territorial clause of the surrender terms stipulated "the terms of the Cairo Declaration shall be carried out and Japanese sovereignty shall be limited to the islands of Honshu, Hokkaido, Kyushu, Shikoku, and such minor islands as we determine." The draft treaty would, in fact, limit Japanese sovereignty accordingly.
>
> The Cairo Declaration provided that "Manchuria, Formosa, and the Pescadores, shall be restored to the Republic of China."
>
> The Government of the United States notes that the remarks of the Soviet Government fail to quote accurately the Cairo Declaration. The word "Manchuria" is deleted and "China" is substituted for "the Republic of China."
>
> . . . in view of the fact that the Government of the Soviet Union has itself pointed out on numerous occasions that the "Republic of China" is not identical with what the Soviet Government now refers to as the "Chinese People's Republic" the Government of the United States inquires of the Government of the Soviet Union whether it in fact now desires that Manchuria, Formosa and the Pescadores should be restored to the "Republic of China."
>
> The draft treaty proceeds on the assumption that Japanese sovereignty "shall be limited" to exclude sovereignty over Formosa and the Pescadores, according to the surrender terms, and that if this is done by Japan, Japan will have done all that can be required of her, and the Japanese people ought not to be denied a state of peace because of a difference of opinion among the Allied powers as to the subsequent disposition of Formosa and the Pescadores.[20]

The United States, besides encountering these expected difficulties with the Soviet Union, met with questioning from Great Britain, some members of the Commonwealth, and some Asian states. Great Britain, in particular, raised the issues of the position of the Chinese Communist regime, of the status of the National Government of China, and of Formosa.

The British attitude was a logical corollary of the

[20] The same, p. 853.

British recognition on January 6, 1950 of the Central People's Government of the People's Republic as the government of China. That action was explained by Prime Minister Atlee, on the occasion of his visit to the United States, in December 1950, on the grounds that the Central People's Government had control of all the mainland of China and commanded the obedience of its inhabitants. He observed that these were stubborn facts, however unpleasant they might be, and he emphasized that Britain was unwilling to cut itself off from one sixth of all the inhabitants of the world and from all chance of making British views known to their rulers. He declared that the British recognition was a recognition of an obvious fact.[21] It has been remarked in various quarters that in this context British expounders of the views and action of the British government make use of the word "recognize" as though it were equivalent to "take cognizance of," whereas to accord *recognition* to a government and to recognize a fact are two very different things.

A joint communiqué issued on December 8 at the conclusion of Mr. Atlee's talks with President Truman made reference to Formosa, as follows:

On the question of Formosa, we have noted that both Chinese claimants have insisted upon the validity of the Cairo Declaration and have expressed reluctance to have the matter considered by the United Nations. We agreed that the issues should be settled by peaceful means and in such a way as to safeguard the interests of the people of Formosa and the maintenance of peace and security in the Pacific, and that consideration of this question by the United Nations will contribute to these ends.[22]

[21] For full text of address given on December 6, 1950 before the National Press Club in Washington, D.C., see *New York Times* (Dec. 7, 1950).

[22] U. S. Department of State, *Bulletin,* Vol. 23 (Dec. 18, 1950), p. 960.

This agreement, which in effect sought to separate the security aspects of the Formosan problem from the problem of deciding between rival claimants to authority in China, left unresolved the differences between the two friendly nations about the more fundamental issue. On April 11, 1951 a Department of State press officer confirmed reports that the United States had received from the British Government an *aide-mémoire* suggesting that the Chinese Communist regime be included in negotiations for a Japanese treaty and that Formosa be returned eventually to "China." Two days later the Department of State issued a statement affirming that it did not contemplate discussions with the Peking regime regarding the Japanese peace settlement but that it had discussed the treaty with the "Republic of China" and had furnished the "National Government" a copy of the draft. It stated further that the United States would continue to follow a policy of opposing the admission of the Peking regime to the United Nations and that United States policy toward Formosa remained as it had been stated repeatedly since the outbreak of aggression in Korea.[23]

British officials expressed the view that the British differences with the United States were being magnified and somewhat misconstrued in public discussions of the subject in the United States. They pointed out that, although Great Britain believed that Communist China should be consulted on the proposed treaty for Japan and that Formosa should eventually be restored to China as provided in the Cairo and the Potsdam declarations, no formal demands had been addressed by the British Government to the United States.[24] Later, on June 14,

[23] The same, Vol. 24 (Apr. 13, 1951).
[24] *Times,* London (Apr. 16, 1951).

official announcement was made in London that full agreement, subject to final approval by the two governments, had been reached in regard to the Japanese peace treaty.[25]

The nature of the agreement thus reached was disclosed in the text of the draft peace treaty with Japan which was jointly prepared and released by the United States and the United Kingdom governments on July 12, 1951. The treaty was signed at San Francisco on September 8 in substantially the form contained in the draft made public on July 12. Article 23 of the treaty provided among other things that the treaty should come into force when instruments of ratification had been deposited by Japan and by a majority, including the United States as the principal occupying power, of the fourteen states specifically listed. China was not included in the list for the reason that no arrangements could be made for that country to participate in the negotiations and become a signatory to the treaty. Although most of the negotiating nations continued to recognize the National Government, several including Great Britain had transferred their recognition to the Peking regime.

Article 25 provided that, for the purposes of the treaty, "the Allied Powers shall be the States at war with Japan, or any State which previously formed a part of the territory of a State named in Article 23, provided that in each case the State concerned has signed and ratified the Treaty." The treaty provided further that, with certain exceptions in favor of China and Korea irrelevant to the present study, the treaty should not confer any rights, titles, or benefits on any state which was not an allied power so defined. Article 26 provided that Japan would be prepared to conclude with any allied power, as de-

[25] U. S. Department of State, *Bulletin,* Vol. 24 (June 25, 1951).

fined in Article 25, that had not become a signatory to the
present treaty, a bilateral treaty of peace on the same or
substantially the same terms as those provided in the
present treaty, but that this obligation on the part of
Japan would expire three years after the coming into
force of the present treaty.[26]

Article 26 means that, although China—represented
by either claimant regime—was excluded as an original
signatory to the treaty, Japan was free to conclude a
separate treaty of peace with either the National Government of China or the Central People's Government.
The only reservation entered was that such a bilateral
treaty, if concluded within three years, must be on substantially the same terms as those of the present multilateral treaty. Presumably a treaty could not be negotiated with the Chinese Communist regime on "substantially the same terms"; and there thus was projected a
three-year period in which to await developments.[27]

The treaty was signed by Japan and forty-eight of the
allied powers. It was not signed by China, the Soviet
Union, Poland, Czechoslovakia, Yugoslavia, Burma, or
India. India, in a note of August 23 to the United States
Government declining to be signatory, gave among other
reasons for its decision the absence in the treaty of provisions for the return of Formosa to China.[28] The American position on this question had been previously stated
by John Foster Dulles in the following terms: "As re-

[26] U. S. Department of State, *Draft Treaty of Peace with Japan* (August 1951).

[27] When queried at San Francisco about the meaning of Article 26,
Premier Yoshida of Japan said, "I don't know whether Japan is in-
vested with the authority to choose between the Chinas or not. I am
inclined to think the question has been shelved for the time being as
one that could not be settled between the United States and Great
Britain." *New York Times* (Sept. 3, 1951).

[28] One June 9, 1952, India concluded a separate peace treaty with
Japan.

gards Formosa, the differences of opinion are such that it could not be definitively dealt with by a Japanese peace treaty to which the Allied powers as a whole are parties. Therefore, the treaty merely takes Japan formally out of the Formosa picture, leaving the position otherwise unchanged."[29]

While this may have been a position satisfactory to the United States as far as the international status of Formosa was concerned, it did not dispose of the more significant question of Formosa as the seat of one of the rival governments of China. Speculation on the action that Japan might take on this question, under Article 26 of the treaty, kept the issue very much alive. In Japan, in Great Britain, and above all in the United States, the question was increasingly pressed as the time for ratifying the treaty drew near. In the course of the resulting discussions, the extensive and perplexing considerations that have entered into all Far Eastern questions for the past three years were brought forcefully to the fore.

The immediate need, from the standpoint of the executive branch of the American government, was to secure the ratification of the treaty by the United States Senate. To this end, the problem of Formosa and the rival governments was presumably carefully examined during the conversations of President Truman and Prime Minister Churchill in January 1952. The extent of the understanding reached is suggested in passages in Churchill's subsequent address to the Congress. In that regard he said:

When I visited Washington during the war I used to be told that China would be one of the Big Four powers among the nations and most friendly to the United States. I was always a bit skeptical. . . .

[29] *New York Times* (Sept. 4, 1951).

You have been wisely resolute, members of the Congress, in confronting Chinese Communist aggression. We take our stand at your side. . . . I am very glad that whatever diplomatic divergencies there may be from time to time about procedure, you do not allow the Chinese anti-communists in Formosa to be invaded and massacred from the mainland.

. . . I congratulate you upon the policy, which in wise and skillful hands, has brought the Japanese nation . . . back to that association with the Western democracies upon which the revowal of their traditions . . . can alone be regained and the stability of the Far East assured.[30]

These remarks, though they indicated no reversal of the original British judgment about the respective importance of the rival claimant governments of China, did represent a closer approach to acceptance of the present American position with respect to the Far East than had hitherto been achieved.

Concurrently, and for the same purpose, the Japanese Government of Premier Yoshida was pressed to declare its intentions under Article 26 of the treaty. Finally, on January 16, 1952 a letter from Premier Yoshida to Ambassador Dulles, dated December 24, 1951, was made public.[31] The essential commitments made therein were as follows:

At the present time it is, we hope, possible to develop that kind of relationship (political peace and commercial intercourse) with the National Government of the Republic of China, which has the seat, voice and vote of China in the United Nations, which exercises actual governmental authority over certain territory, and which maintains diplomatic relations with most of the members of the United Nations.

My government is prepared as soon as legally possible to conclude with the National Government of China, if that government so desires, a Treaty which will establish normal relations . . . in conformity with the principles set out

[30] *New York Times* (Jan. 18, 1952).
[31] U. S. Department of State, Press Release 37 (Jan. 16, 1952).

in the multilateral Treaty of Peace. The terms of such
bilateral treaty shall, in respect of the Republic of China,
be applicable to all territories which are now, or which
may hereafter be, under the control of the National Government of China.

As regards the Chinese Communist regime, that regime
stands actually condemned by the United Nations of being
an aggressor and, in consequence, the United Nations has
recommended certain measures against that regime, in which
Japan is now concurring and expects to continue to concur.
. . . Furthermore, the Sino-Soviet Treaty . . . concluded in
Moscow in 1950 is virtually a military alliance aimed against
Japan. In fact there are many reasons to believe that the
Communist regime in China is backing the Japanese Communist Party in its program of seeking violently to overthrow the constitutional system and the present Government of Japan. In view of these considerations, I can assure
you that the Japanese government has no intention to
conclude a bilateral treaty with the Communist regime of
China.

This letter defined a Japanese position in a way that
raised for future consideration international questions
as numerous as were those which, among those that had
been pending, it settled to the satisfaction of the United
States. It clearly adopted the American position in regard
to Chinese representation in the United Nations. The
letter recognized the claim to ultimate authority of the
National Government of China by referring not only to
the territory now under Nationalist control (Formosa)
but to territories "which may hereafter be" under the
control of that government. The Central People's Government of China was defined as an active enemy of
Japan, a position that was more than the minimum required to identify Japan with the anti-Communist nations. Moreover that position linked a concurrence in the
action of the United Nations against the Chinese Communists with the concern of the Japanese Government
regarding the problem of Japan's national security.

At this point, the problem in relation to Formosa that arose and was handled in the United Nations and the problem in relation to Formosa that arose and was handled in connection with the Japanese Peace Treaty merged and became a focal point in any broad adjustment that might be sought in the Far East.

The Japanese Peace Treaty, having become ratified by the requisite number of powers, came into force on April 28, 1952. On the same day, a treaty of peace between the governments of Japan and of the Republic of China was signed at Taipei. In an exchange of notes between the plenipotentiaries accompanying the treaty of peace, there was confirmed the understanding reached that the terms of the treaty "shall, in respect to the Republic of China, be applicable to all the territories which are now, or *which may hereafter be,* under the control of its government."[32] Thus speculation on the action that Japan might take with regard to China was set at rest.

[32] Italics supplied.

PART THREE

THE PRESENT AND
THE FUTURE

CHAPTER 9.

The Present Situation

THE Second World War thrust Formosa for the first time into the orbit of United States interest and concern. Postwar developments in China, with the resulting withdrawal (in 1949) of the National Government to Formosa, brought into existence the "problem of Formosa" with which the United States is now inevitably confronted. It seems idle to speculate at this late date whether, if the United States had pursued a different policy toward China between, say, 1944 and 1949, the problem would not have arisen. At any rate, a solution now appears not likely to be reached except as an integral and consistent part of a comprehensive Far Eastern settlement. Such a settlement will probably have to await either a marked shift in the present balance of power among the nations ranged by conflicting interests and objectives on opposing sides, or by the reaching of a conclusion by either or both sides that their interests can better be served by an accommodation than by adhering rigidly to their present positions.

Neither of these eventualities is likely to occur soon, and neither side is strong enough to warrant its assuming the risks of attempting to coerce the other. Consequently, the prospect is that there will be a stalemate of indefinite duration, with a continuance of a somewhat precarious *status quo*. In the meantime, measures taken by the United States to deal with the problem of Formosa will tend to be on a short-term basis in order that the carrying out of whatever long-term disposals may in the future be decided upon as being in the best interests of the United States will not be prejudiced. Furthermore, it is conceivable that a collapse of the negotiations for a truce in Korea might produce repercussions in the United States which would precipitate American action against Communist China of a nature that would profoundly affect the future basis of American policy with regard to Formosa.

For the present, it is worthwhile to try to define the position in which the United States now stands with respect to the problem of Formosa. As has been shown in previous chapters, the present position is compounded of many different elements. It was created out of the fragments of a disintegrating relationship with the National Government of China, out of an expanding policy of containing and then of positively opposing the threat of Communist aggression, out of the immediate political and military requirements of a war in the Far East, out of a desire to lay some new basis for stability there, and out of the necessities as well as the frustrations of trying to organize and carry out a procedure of collective action. Above all, it was reached under the persistent pressure of an American attitude and public opinion which, in turn, was being shaped and reshaped by the strong winds of political controversy and by sharp reactions to the failure of events to fulfill preconceived expectations.

If the present position can be defined, it then becomes possible to examine its constituent parts and to suggest that some parts may be more fundamental than others; that some may constitute essential commitments of the

United States while others are merely manifestations of
public impatience to reach quick and final solutions;
and, again, that some parts represent a significant direction in policy while others will be recognized as leading
into blind alleys. Until the existing situation is precisely
defined, its unresolved elements cannot be clearly identified nor can the possible future questions implicit in
the situation be formulated.

Choices Presented to the United States
at the Close of 1949

The specific wartime commitment of the United
States with respect to Formosa—that contained in the
Cairo Declaration—was implemented when American
forces assisted the National Government of China to
receive the Japanese surrender and to reoccupy the
island. The step remaining to be taken was the conversion of China's *de facto* authority in Formosa into
de jure sovereignty, through formalization in a peace
treaty with Japan. It had not been foreseen that before
a peace treaty could be concluded Formosa would be
the only part of China still under the control of the
National Government. When that government lost its
authority on the mainland, in December 1949, the
United States found itself with no prepared policy as a
basis for action.

The American Government and public opinion were
unable to come to a speedy agreement on what should
be done. The Government was faced with a dilemma.
On the one hand, it had already announced clearly
that American aid to the National Government of
China had been of no avail, and that nothing that the
United States could have done within the reasonable

limits of its capabilities would have changed the result (Communist domination on mainland China). On the other hand, it had committed itself deeply to containing the further expansion of Soviet communism. These two positions were brought into conflict in China.

The United States Government was unwilling to give further active support to the National Government in its efforts to maintain itself; yet public opinion would not permit official recognition of the exercise of authority by the Central People's Government. The United States proposed to uphold, however, the claim of the National Government to continue to represent China in the Security Council and in other organs of the United Nations and was prepared to oppose efforts to have the credentials of the Nationalist representatives transferred to representatives of the Central People's Government. The American Government did not intend to entertain claims to consideration by a Communist regime that had established itself by subversion and force; but it would not commit itself to aiding the undeniably anti-Communist opponent in China of that regime in its effort to survive. Finally the United States, which earlier had had no doubts about the international status and the ultimate disposal of Formosa to the Republic of China, was now confronted with a situation in which neither public opinion nor the security interests of the United States would permit passive acquiescence in a Communist occupation of Formosa or the taking of a course that might facilitate consolidation of the authority of the People's Government.

At the outset of 1950, the American Government had before it a choice among three possible courses of action. It might reverse its earlier decision not to support the National Government and proceed at least with steps to enable that government to maintain itself in Formosa. It might push its earlier decision to a positive conclusion —one which the British regarded as "realistic"—namely, to recognize the Chinese Communist regime and formulate a new policy on that basis. Or, it might postpone making a choice between those two courses while continuing to act in a way that would at least close to future action no doors that were still open.

It was the third of these courses that was adopted, under pressure of events, at the outset of the year 1950. Earlier, in October 1949, the Administration had announced that it would not recognize the Communist regime without first consulting the Congress of the United States, where voiced sentiment was preponderantly against such a step. It announced, in January 1950. that no military aid—not even advisory—would be given to the National Government and that the United States would not interfere in the "civil conflict" in China. Yet economic aid continued to be given on Formosa, and ultimately military aid was also given.

In view of the uncertainties of the international situation then prevailing, of the relative weakness of the United States in terms of its mobilized resources compared with those of the Soviet Union, and of the uncrystallized state of American public opinion, a case can perhaps be made for the decision to stand by and "let the dust settle." Certainly there were elements in the situation that were not likely to respond in their entirety to any single course of action that the United States could have taken. The course of the Communist advance could not have been checked without a major effort. In the light of its past performance, the National Government offered a foundation of doubtful value on which to try to rebuild an American position in the Far

East. Neither the status of Formosa, which had been only loosely determined by international agreement, nor the position of China in the United Nations could be fixed with finality by unilateral action on the part of the United States. And above all, the situation itself was so fluid that an attempt at final judgment on any of these matters might well have seemed unjustified.

On the other hand, a case might be made with no less cogency, both on moral grounds and on grounds of long-term and abiding concepts and objectives, against the course which the United States took. On moral grounds, the United States might have been less assailable for the policies which it adopted had it not been for the part which its representatives had played at Yalta and for the steps which it took later to bring about a Nationalist-Communist coalition, and had American officials not been voluble in their public criticisms—however well founded—of the Chinese Government and its officials. It is contended that by the leadership which it had attempted to exercise in China, the United States had incurred an inescapable share in the responsibility for the consequences, which were a weakening of the National Government and the prejudicing of its position in the minds of the Chinese people.

In defending President Truman's decision of January 5, 1950, that the United States would withhold military aid from the Nationalist forces in Formosa, Secretary Acheson spoke of the need for safeguarding confidence in our motivation so as to ensure concentration of Chinese wrath not on us but on the Soviet Union. Such a course, however, can have served little practical purpose if at the same time it resulted in the loss to the Chinese people of the means whereby they might eventually regain the national independence and personal liberties of which Communist imperialism had in effect deprived them. Contrariwise, were Formosa denied to the Communists, the island might continue to be a haven for the National Government. And that government, by seizing the opportunity thus presented to develop enlightened political institutions, would remain a symbol to all non-Communist Chinese, both at home and abroad, of the continuity of their national life as a free nation, and would persist as a rallying point for future resistance by them to an alien domination of their country. Formosa might then likewise be a channel for outside contact with the Chinese people, and aid rendered there by the United States would signalize to that people the abiding character of American friendship and the traditional desire of the United States to see that China survived and its people's rights were respected. This aspect of the matter seems either to have been overlooked or, having been considered, to have been regarded as of less importance than the considerations in favor of taking the wait-and-see course that was initially adopted.

In any event, and in spite of vigorous criticism, six months elapsed after the retreat, in December 1949, of the National Government to Formosa, before the American Government came to a revision of its position.

Present Objectives of American Policy

When in June 1950 the North Korean Communists invaded the Republic of Korea and the United Nations opposed this act of armed aggression, the necessity of meeting the crisis with affirmative measures ruled out any further waiting on developments. This does not mean that, at that point, the United States cast the die unalterably in favor of support of the National Government. Rather, the decision to "neutralize" Formosa can best be understood if the purposes expressed in the President's announcement are taken literally: "In these circumstances the occupation of Formosa by Communist forces would be a direct threat to the security of the Pacific area and to United States forces performing their necessary and lawful functions in that area." The United States Government for its part was willing to let matters rest for the time being with the announced interposition of the Seventh Fleet.

The United States did not, however, control all the elements and factors in the situation. Many of its fellow-members in the United Nations had regarded the attitude of the United States toward the Formosa question as both confused and unstable, and many viewed the reference to "neutralization" of the island as an unwelcome sign that American policy was committing the United States to a division of attention and effort, whereas the exigencies of the United Nations commitment in Korea called for concentration on the problem of defeating the enemy there.

Meanwhile the National Government, which had steadily maintained that a war in the Far East was inevitable and that its position would be restored as part of such a conflict, offered—as a member of the United Nations—33,000 of its troops for service in Korea. The offer was refused, on the advice of the American Joint Chiefs of Staff, on the ground that these troops could function more effectively in the defense of Formosa. Political considerations arising from an unwillingness to leave the relatively safe ground of "neutralization" might also have entered into the decisions of the United States Government on this matter.

The course of the war in Korea and the intervention of the Chinese Communists late in 1950 made it increasingly difficult for the United States Government to maintain its delicately balanced position between opposing views. The major pressure for a change came from American public opinion, and the Government was slowly but surely moved in the direction of committing itself to the National Government of China. The steps by which policy was crystallized were small and tentative, and each step was taken with a backward look; but all steps were in the same direction.

A re-examination at this point of the sections of this study that deal with the development of United States policy toward Formosa and with the new grants of military assistance to the National Government will show the rate at which the movement to a new position progressed. Now the purport of American policy is being expressed in terms of (1) effort to prevent Formosa from falling into Communist hands; and (2) support of the National Government of China.

However simple and limited these indications of objectives may seem to be when viewed in the context of the current conflict in the Far East, they have wide-ranging implications when considered in the light of existing international relations broadly viewed. These implications strongly suggest that the problem of Formosa has not necessarily been settled because American policy toward Formosa has been defined with some degree of clarity.

It is likely that service of the first objective—to keep Formosa from falling to the Chinese Communists—will for the moment, and in the absence of any Communist effort to attack the island, be assured by the presence of American naval and air strength in or near the Formosan Straits. It is a fact that the capacity of the National Government to defend itself in Formosa is being built up by military aid and advice, and it may be assumed that this is a strong deterrent to a Communist operation against the island.

It is the serving of the second objective—that of supporting the National Government—that is fraught with ambiguities and uncertainties. Support of the National Government has minimum and maximum connotations. At the minimum it can mean merely providing what is required in the way of equipment and other resources to hold the island against even a major attack. At the maximum it can mean a series of interrelated supporting actions designed to further the efforts of the National Government to establish a firm economic base and to help it develop its Formosan seat into a community that may prove to be a model for Asia and constitute a continuing threat to the claim of the Chinese Communists to speak for and represent China.

It is impossible at the present moment to judge where, along this scale between minimum and maximum connotations, American policy now stands. American action in the course of two years (1951-52) has, however, carried support of the National Government to a point that is closer to the maximum connotation of a policy of support than to the minimum. The economic condition of Formosa has steadily improved in spite of the heavy burdens that have been imposed on the island's limited resources. A surprising degree of social and political stability has been achieved through administrative reforms, through increased governmental efficiency, and through the progressive solution of local problems. Contrary to some expectations and predictions, the National Government is a "going concern" with a reasonably well-organized territorial base. Moreover, the National Government, firmly supported by the United States, represents China in the United Nations. The cumulative effect of these items of support has been that the National Government of China is an influential factor in international affairs to an extent beyond its actual power and resources.

In the American view there have of course been practical short-term benefits from the policy that has brought the National Government to its present situation. Formosa has not been attacked. A rallying point for all non-Communist Chinese has been maintained and strengthened. A legitimate authority, representing a lawful succession of Chinese governments and a continuity in the national life of the Chinese people as a free people, has been preserved as a tangible alternative to recognition of the present Communist regime. Finally, another focal point of resistance to communism in Eastern Asia—in addition to Korea and Indo-China and Malaya—has been established. While some of these benefits may have largely a symbolic value at the present moment, and while the importance of these symbolic values can be and frequently is overestimated, they do have a usefulness that should not be disregarded.

The current trend of American opinion on the significance of Formosa in relation to possible future action toward combating the advance of militant communism is reflected in the visit of inspection to the Island early in May 1952, of Admiral Arthur W. Radford, United States Commander-in-Chief in the Pacific, and in his statements in a press conference there. He is said to have emphasized the importance of Formosa as a vital link in the Western Pacific defense chain and as a factor in planning for defense against further Communist aggression. Referring to a possible naval blockade of Communist China he expressed the view that such a blockade would only be ordered in an effort to halt further Communist aggression—and then only as a part of the total action to be taken to halt it.[1]

In considering the significance of this trend and its possible projection, one of the proposals that emerged from the conversation between President Truman and Prime Minister Churchill in January 1952 needs to be noted. If, as was then suggested, the Chinese Communist regime were to be notified that a further act of aggression on its part or a breaking of any truce that might be agreed upon in Korea would subject it and its territory to direct retaliation, the National Government of China, its base on Formosa, and its military resources would come clearly into the purview of the available means of acting on the warning.

It is obvious that, as of May 1952, the trend that has been described has not been developed in all or even in most of its aspects. That it will be further developed is, however, implicitly indicated in many of the steps that have been taken by the United States during the past twelve months. But, since there are factors in the situation as it now stands over which the United States cannot exercise control or influence sufficient to enable it to determine the way in which they will operate, the ultimate objective of American policy for Formosa remains but vaguely defined, and the direction of American action in regard to Formosa is not yet conclusively set.

[1] *New York Times* (May 8, 1952).

CHAPTER 10.

The Unresolved Questions

A T THE moment of concluding this study, it is to be noted that the short-term objective of the policy that the United States has developed with respect to Formosa is being achieved. Formosa was to be kept from falling into unfriendly hands. This has been done, and by means that have entailed relatively little drain on American resources in short supply—military man power and modern weapons. It has been done by economic aid and by military assistance which have facilitated the efforts of the National Government to carry out political and economic reforms and to improve its capacity for self-defense. It has been done also by "neutralizing" Formosa at a critical period and by thus robbing the project of seizing the island by force of all of its allure.

Differences of opinion on the strategic importance of Formosa need not be argued. Whatever the strategic value, that value is being preserved for the time being, and can continue to be preserved as long as the aims of American policy call for allocation of the necessary means and as long as the American tax payer is willing to foot the bill. The probable future requirements of preserving this value constitute, however, one of the unresolved questions to be examined.

More important than the question of the continued

willingness of the American Government and public to bear the cost of keeping Formosa in friendly hands are the questions that arise out of the political dilemmas created for American policy by the measures that have been adopted to achieve this purpose. The policy of helping to defend Formosa by supporting the National Government was developed in an atmosphere of domestic and international controversy. The political overtones of those disagreements are still factors in the problem of Formosa. These overtones reflect profound disagreements over the international position of the National Government of China, over the strength and the reliability of the Kuomintang, which dominates that government, over the status of Formosa, and over the real significance of the revolutionary process that is taking place in the Far East. In the judgment of the governments of some friendly nations and in the opinion of many Americans, the present policy of the United States has unilaterally foreclosed, by implication at least, the resolving of some of these points of difference. Contrariwise, in the judgment of other friendly states and in the opinion of many other Americans, the present policy has not gone far enough in giving an unequivocal answer on the points at issue.

Although these differences are momentarily quiescent, the possibility cannot be overlooked that the People's Government of China might at any time take action that would bring these differences to the fore again. A threat of new aggression might easily force American policy far along the road which it has tentatively entered, especially if the threat were directed at Formosa and probably also if directed at Indo-China. Out of this possibility there arises a second set of unresolved questions.

The third, and perhaps the most significant question

affects the character of the ultimate objectives of the United States in the Far East and therefore the substance of its foreign policy. The question relates to the relative importance to be assigned to the objective of preserving Formosa as a base for the National Government—as a means, among several means, of serving over-all United States interests in the Far East. This question arises because it might conceivably be found that the pursuit of this objective conflicted with other objectives, such as the effectuation of a settlement in Korea and the establishment of more friendly relations with India and perhaps other Asian countries, or it might be found that the policy can be further pursued only at a very burdensome cost.

The answer to this question will depend upon estimates in regard to the future such as: the ultimate prospects for the re-establishment of a friendly and non-Communist regime on the Chinese mainland, and the prospective value to the United States of having in China an ally instead of an enemy as compared with the value of other alignments whose effectuation might be prejudiced by American efforts to preserve the National Government. Until such judgments can safely be reached with an approach to finality, this question will remain unresolved.

The Internal Problem of Formosa

The internal problem of Formosa arises from the fact that the island, with a population and resources that are insignificant in comparison with those of the Chinese mainland, is unable by itself to support the role in which it has been cast by events. Continuing aid from the United States is essential if the gap between what the resources of the island afford and the civil and military requirements is to be kept closed.

Formosa has substantial resources, an industrious population, and a geographical position favorable to the development of foreign trade. But, quite aside from the threat of a Communist attack, there has devolved upon Formosa—the smallest of China's provinces—the burden of maintaining the operations of the National Government, including keeping armed forces on a war footing, and of supporting a million refugees from the mainland.

Thus far, the National Government has kept its head above water not only by accepting and using American aid but also by drawing heavily on its gold and foreign exchange reserves. In spite of the success with which the productive capacity of Formosa has been reorganized—by the combined efforts of the people, the government, and the Economic Cooperation Administration—the outlook for the future is problematic. Formosa cannot be expected to be self-supporting as long as the National Government is called upon to exhaust its own reserves and to draw heavily upon the resources of the island to maintain an organized defense against a possible assault.

The matter goes deeper than that. The National Government of China still hopes to regain its position on the mainland. To be sure, there is no evidence that any active preparations are under way to achieve it. Indeed, the National Government, with only Formosa at its disposal, clearly lacks the means to carry out such an undertaking. If, however, such a project were to be undertaken, the acquiring of additional resources in the form of outside assistance essential for this purpose would depend upon the extent to which the purposes of the National Government would appear to be identical with the interests of some allied nation that might make up the difference. For the moment, the United States alone could be that other nation.

Doubts arise, however, as estimates of possibilities are projected into the future. It cannot be assumed that a comprehensive settlement of the power conflict in the Far East will be rapidly reached. It cannot be assumed that the resources of the National Government of China, unless that government should succeed in reinstating itself on the mainland, can ever become adequate for the role which has been cast for it and which it aspires to play in the Far East. The present prospect is that the United States will need to continue to subsidize, in some way or other, the National Government and to underwrite at least part of the costs of maintaining Nationalist China's Formosan base.

American policy now operates in three ways in this situation. Economic aid is directed to increasing the productive capacity of Formosa. Military assistance is directed toward improving the defensive capabilities of the Nationalist army.[1] The United States, by interposing the Seventh Fleet between the island and the mainland of China, has measurably improved the defensive position of the National Government. The present state of American opinion clearly supports these measures and, far from objecting to the cost involved, is inclined to press for additional measures the adoption of which must necessarily involve an increase in expenditures.

How long, however, and how far would this support continue to be given? The question would be posed in an acute form if American policy were to call upon the

[1] The extent to which military assistance is also being used to develop the offensive capabilities of these forces is not known.

National Government to take the offensive against the
Chinese Communists, or in the perhaps still more unlikely event that the National Government were to take
the initiative in this matter and thus present the United
States with a difficult choice between supporting what
might otherwise turn out to be a fiasco or taking the
risk that Nationalist China be wiped out and Formosa
be occupied by the Communists.

The question could arise from less drastic developments: those of a continuing drain on American resources, scrutinized by the Congress with increasing dis-
taste as a commitment competing with other commitments of American resources. Subsidies to foreign states
are notoriously displeasing to legislators in a democracy,
and indefinitely repeated appropriations for aid that appears to be unproductive of positive results beyond
maintaining a *status quo* are soon identified by democratic opinion as a subsidy.

On the other hand, there also have to be taken into
account other possibilities, however remote they may
appear at the moment. The grip on China of the Communist regime might weaken, and widespread uprisings
might occur, offering promise, with some outside aid,
of a successful revolt. It is conceivable also that even in
the absence of an armed revolt a process of distintegra-
tion may set in after the initial impetus of Communist
successes in China has spent its force. Or, the Chinese
economy might go from bad to worse in consequence of
one or more depressive developments. Or, some other
turn of events might create a favorable opportunity for
the Chinese Nationalists to deal the Communist regime
an ultimately decisive blow.

It is considerations such as these that make the possibility of maintaining the viability of Formosa an open question. The present reasonably satisfactory condition of the island is misleading. The basic weaknesses in the situation are not plainly visible, and the fact that a breathing spell has developed has given rise to optimistic estimates. The situation could, however, on very short notice, take a turn for the worse.

The International Dilemmas

While it is now the policy of the United States to give aid to the National Government of China toward maintaining the internal economy of Formosa and toward defending that island, the United States does not have complete freedom of action in implementing this policy. It must take account of the interests and the views of the free nations with which it is associated, and it must give heed to the effect of its actions in Formosa upon other important American interests and objectives.

These limitations play a part in connection with consideration of each of three unresolved questions. These questions are: (1) the international position of the National Government of China; or, more precisely, Chinese representation in the United Nations; (2) the status of Formosa; and (3) the basis for stabilizing the Far East. There are, of course, irreconcilable differences between the Soviet-Communist bloc and the free nations on each of these questions. What is perhaps even more significant is the fact that the free nations themselves do not stand on a common ground with respect to any of them. Both of these sets of differences enter into the deliberations of the United Nations. Therefore, unless the United States proposes to move unilaterally to achieve its objectives, it will have to be prepared to effect adjustments when persuasion fails to enlist the support of other powers.

Some of the nations even most friendly to the United States have occasionally felt that American policy toward Formosa and toward the National Government was prejudicial to establishing a basis for stabilizing the Far East. If, for example, the United States were to become increasingly committed to strengthening the National Government of China, this would tend to freeze the position of the United States on the question of the place of that government in the United Nations and on the question of the disposal of Formosa. Moreover, some other powers might see in the adoption of such a course an implication that the United States regarded the elimination of the Communist regime in China, or, stated differently, the reinstatement of a non-Communist regime on the Chinese mainland, as a prerequisite to the restoration of stability in the Far East. Yet, all of these questions may be considered to be open questions insofar as an international decision is concerned.

It is in this area of uncertainty and doubt that unresolved political dilemmas can reappear in connection with the problem of Formosa. How far can the United States develop its support of the National Government of China without inviting counter-measures by Communist China? How soon would apprehensions arise in India, in Siam, in Burma and in Indonesia that what they might regard as "an unwarranted war" was in the making? How soon would these apprehensions build up into a concerted effort, through the United Nations and other channels, to restrain the United States? At that point, would the United States stand flatly on its own judgment, or would it modify its policy until a common ground was found?

Again, although some Asian governments and peoples —not only the Chinese Nationalists but the Japanese, the South Koreans, and the Filipinos—favor a strong course against Communist China, other non-Communist Asian countries hold a different view of the events that have taken place in China and are not now disposed to support a policy that has apparent to them no other purpose than to oppose Communism. In the eyes of such governments, Asian nationalism, while it may be threatened by Communism, sometimes seems to be even more seriously threatened by a Western policy of conducting a determined struggle against Asian Communism (that is, Communism in Asia). In this view, peace at almost any price might appear preferable to involvement in a conflict that may check national development and might well result in the re-establishment of some new form of Western "colonialism."

The exponents of such attitudes are likely to be extremely critical of the actions of the United States in the Far East. In some important respects, the form and the methods of American policy toward Formosa and the National Government have become a kind of touchstone. Out of this arises another sort of unresolved political dilemma. This dilemma can be stated as: Can the United States act in Formosa in a way that will achieve the purposes of its present policy but will not arouse antagonisms among substantial sections of Asian opinion and thus deprive it of a foundation for a more comprehensive and longer-term policy for stabilizing the Far East?

The difficulties of working a way out of this dilemma

are as numerous as the proposals for resolving it, since no course of action can be wholly free from offense and at the same time satisfy the demands of American opinion for prompt and positive results.

The Status of the National Government and of Formosa

We must go back for a moment to consider the two questions in which other free nations than those of Asia are concerned: the status of the National Government and the status of the area within which it governs. The essential facts are reasonably clear. Differences arise from the interpretation of the facts. In both cases, the interpretation that has been made by the United States has no binding force unless it is accepted and acted upon by the free nations of the world and by majority opinion in the United Nations.

Pertinent facts regarding the status of the National Government are as follows: it is a government; it is Chinese; it exercises effective authority in one of the provinces of China; it is looked upon by many Chinese as the government of China; and it has been and is "recognized" by more than half of the states of the world as the lawful government of the Republic of China. When, in 1945, the Republic of China was recognized as a major power and was assigned a permanent seat in the Security Council of the United Nations, it was the National Government that sat and spoke in the name of China. That right has since been questioned by the Soviet Union and some other states and has, up to the present time, been successfully defended by the American and various other governments. Neither the Security Council nor the General Assembly has seen fit to act in the matter, to withdraw the privilege of a permanent seat in the Security Council, or to question the credentials of representatives from the National Government to the other organs of the United Nations. For some time, the United States Government has taken a firm position on the matter.[2] But these facts will continue to govern the situation only so long as the other members of the United Nations continue to think and act as they have done up to this time.

Pertinent facts concerning the status of Formosa are as follows: The Cairo Declaration stated that Formosa should be returned to the Republic of China; the Japanese forces on Formosa surrendered by agreement to the forces of the Republic of China, and the National Government assumed authority over the island. This *de facto* establishment of Chinese authority was not questioned at the time or later up to 1950 by any of the powers, but it was tacitly understood that the *de jure* status of Formosa would be subject to confirmation in a treaty. This reservation was not formally assented to by the National Government. As the conflict between the National Government and the Communist Party in China progressed, it became evident that it might become possible to contend that the National Government had ceased to be the Government of China. Ultimately, although the majority of the states which composed the Family of Nations still recognize it as the Government of the Republic of China, no one contends that it is the Government of the "People's Republic of China" (a political entity created and proclaimed by the Com-

[2] Secretary of State Acheson, on June 2, 1951, told the members of the Armed Services and of the Foreign Relations committees of the Senate that the United States had successfully opposed and would continue to oppose the seating of the Chinese Communist regime in the United Nations. He added that the United States had a just cause, had persuasive advocates, and would continue to have a great majority of the nations on its side. See, *Military Situation in the Far East*, Hearings before the Senate Committee on Armed Services and the Committee on Foreign Relations, 82 Cong. 1 sess. (1951), p. 1755.

munists).[3] However, the National Government did survive and, moreover, established its seat on Formosa. The
situation then became one in which two questions were
involved. The first was whether or not the right of
China to Formosa should be confirmed. The second was,
if it were confirmed, which of the claimant Chinese
governments was to be regarded as the rightful one. At
that point, the issue of the status of Formosa became
inextricably linked with that of the status of the National Government of the Republic of China.

International opinion divided in several ways, and
surprising alignments were made and unmade as events
in the Far East suggested the advisability of keeping the
situation fluid. American policy, however, tended to
freeze the situation. The Government of the United
States asserted that it recognized "the National Government of the Republic of China even though the territory
under its control is severely restricted." The Government of the United States also said, referring to the
peace treaty with Japan, "the treaty merely takes Japan
formally out of the Formosa picture, leaving the position
otherwise unchanged."[4] In effect, these statements taken
together seem to mean that in the American view the
former sovereignty of Japan over Formosa is definitely
annulled and that the transfer of the sovereignty to the
National Government is recognized. Needless to say,
the first part of this position is presumably accepted by
at least the signatories of the treaty, but the second part
is supported only by the facts of the present situation and

[3] Some governments, notably those that have backed the Chinese
Communists, have denied the validity of the reservation so as to
strengthen the claim of the Communist regime to be the Government
of China. Other governments, notably that of the United States, have
upheld the reservation primarily out of fairness to the allied powers that
had not been party to the Cairo Declaration.

[4] See above, pp. 119, 157.

the willingness of the American Government to use the power of the United States to back up its view. Thus, in essence, the issue of the status of Formosa has become identical with the issue of the international position of the National Government, and both are equally subject to the resolving of the internal struggle for the control of China and to the crystallizing of international sentiment regarding the significance and the consequences of this struggle.

In this sense also, the status of Formosa must be regarded as a question that is not definitely resolved. The position that the United States has apparently taken may be unequivocal in American eyes, but it still leaves many loose ends internationally. The extent to which it will be supported by the other members of the United Nations is not clear. The extent to which even American policy may or may not develop the implications of this position into a comprehensive Far Eastern policy is equally uncertain.

It is important to remember, when trying to assess further possibilities in these respects, that the problem of Formosa is linked with the effort to reach a settlement in Korea and with an interest in preventing further aggression by the Chinese Communist regime. It is well to recall here that, although the present policy of the United States toward Formosa was in a substantial degree shaped by events in Korea, the basis of the United Nations action in Korea was not conditioned in any significant way by events in Formosa. Thus, while it may be important to the United States to keep the development of an armistice in Korea absolutely divorced from the question of Formosa, it is equally important to the Chinese Communists to bring the two together; and, to many members of the United Nations, the

American position regarding Formosa might be made to appear prejudicial to the effort to achieve a settlement in Korea.

In these circumstances, the United Nations could conceivably reach the conclusion that achievement of peace and security in the Far East depends upon trans-ferring China's seat in the United Nations from the National Government to the Central People's Government, determining that *de jure* authority over Formosa is similarly transferred, and calling for a comprehensive adjustment of the situation in the Far East on that basis. The slightest tendency of international opinion to move in that direction might put the United Staes in a difficult position.[5] Presumably the United States would expect to exert its influence in the United Nations and among the free nations individually to ensure international support for the American position.

If a reasoned approach should fail to persuade the majority of free nations of the merits of the American position, the United States would then be faced with two choices. One choice would be, in the interests of

[5] Some authorities on international law argue that the United States would still remain free to regard the National Government as the government of China and to consider Formosa a part of that China of which the National Government was in its opinion still the *de jure* government. These authorities add that, alternatively, the United States might maintain that the status of Formosa still remained to be settled by a multilateral international agreement. In either case, such authorities say, the United States would be legally entitled to give military assistance to the National Government on the ground that it was the *de jure* government of a friendly state. Proponents of these views further argue that the boundaries of Communist China would not automatically be determined by a vote to seat the Central People's Government in the United Nations in place of the National Government. This would be a separate and a substantive question, and action upon it would be subject to a veto in the Security Council. No matter how sound this opinion may be, it might not prevent the United States from finding itself in an isolated position internationally.

safeguarding objectives elsewhere, to make concessions with regard to Formosa. The other would be, as a means of having the American position with regard to Formosa prevail, to resort either to unilateral action or to the exertion of extraordinary pressure upon friendly nations, thereby endangering the maintaining of concert with them in the pursuit of objectives elsewhere.[6]

Such, in brief, is the dilemma which the problem of Formosa poses to the United States in its wider international relations. The question, therefore, of the relationship of the problem of Formosa to the problem of a policy for promoting stability in the Far East becomes a subject of major importance.

Formosa and the Problem of Far Eastern Policy

During and after the Second World War, under the stress of military exigencies in the China theater and of unprecedented postwar conditions, there were deviations made from the historic Far Eastern policy of the United States. It is at least arguable that many of the

[6] Still another issue regarding the international status of Formosa, which at one time had been posed, might be revived in the future under certain conceivable circumstances. It will be recalled that in the early part of 1950, some of the proponents in the United States of a policy of preventing Formosa from falling into Chinese Communist hands expressed doubt whether this should be achieved by supporting the National Government of China or the establishment on the island of an independent government based on the local population (which is almost entirely Chinese). After the outbreak in June 1950 of Communist aggression in Korea, that question was for the time being disposed of, in favor of supporting the National Government. However, should the National Government, either upon its own initiative or at the instance of the United States, embark upon a military expedition for the purpose of reinstating itself on the mainland, and should the expedition end in disaster, the issue of supporting an independent Formosa as an alternative means of keeping Formosa in friendly hands would be likely to come to the fore again. The merits of such a course would necessarily have to be weighed in the light of the then existing surrounding circumstances.

difficulties that today lie in the way of furthering constant and long-range American objectives are the direct consequence of American actions which were inconsistent with the principles underlying traditional American policy. This is not to suggest, however, that by now going back to traditional policy the evils that have thus befallen the United States and other countries could be remedied. But it is clear at least that the modifications of earlier policy that were introduced, especially after 1944, have not contributed to serve American best interests, and this modified policy has become inoperable in detail. It is probable that some new general policy is in process of evolving. Consequently, the position of the United States in the Far East is in a fluid state, and its ultimate objectives are not clearly formulated. In these circumstances, policy is subject to shifts under the influence of passing events, short-term purposes, and demands for *ad hoc* disposals.

On one aspect, however, policy seems to have reached a fairly firm position—with respect to Formosa. In comparison with other aspects of policy in relation to the Far East, the purposes and actions of the United States have been so sharply defined that apprehensions might be entertained by some lest ultimately American interests and objectives in relation to the Far East as a whole be subordinated to those in Formosa. Whether such apprehensions would be justified or not, time alone can tell. This would depend upon whether the People's Government remains a fixture in China and succeeds in reconciling the Chinese people to its exercise of authority or whether American policy proves to be instrumental in preserving Formosa as a base for the recovery of the Chinese mainland by a future government that would represent the free choice of the Chinese people. In the latter eventuality, since China, because of its central position in the Far East and its vast area and population, is the key to the stability of the Far East, one might wonder whether these considerations had not intuitively underlain the attitude of the American public on the Formosan question.

At any rate, the way in which the United States now develops its position with regard to Formosa and to relations with the National Government can have profound repercussions throughout the Far East. Conversely, developments in any one of a number of areas in the Far East—for example in Korea or in Indo-China —can pose for American policy toward Formosa very difficult choices. In either case, American action and its consequences are likely to have a fundamentally determining effect on the ultimate pattern of American and Western relations with the Far East.

It was observed earlier in this analysis that American policy toward Formosa had taken a direction that might lead to the acceptance by the United States of some very onerous commitments. This is of course only a possibility. Not all of the American eggs are being carried in the Formosan basket, though the temptation so to proceed can easily become strong. Some sections of American opinion find the temptation almost irresistible and propose over and over that the Communist regime in China be challenged by the counter-revolutionary forces of the National Government.[7] Such proposals carry con-

---

[7] General MacArthur, when he received orders in June 1950 calling for the "neutralization" of Formosa recommended that "the wraps be taken off the Generalissimo, that he be furnished with such logistic support as would put those [the Nationalist] troops in fighting trim and that he be permitted to use his own judgment as to their use. The slightest use that was made of those troops would have taken the pressure off my troops [in Korea]. It would have saved me thousands of lives up there even a threat of that." *Military Situation in the Far East*, Hearings, p. 22.

Chiang Kai-shek is reported to have said in an interview with the

siderable weight because they are invariably presented in terms of American security. To act on them, however, would result in making the present Formosan policy of the United States govern its Far Eastern policy.

In effect, it would commit the United States to seeing that the National Government succeeds in its effort to regain its authority on the Chinese mainland, and the possible extent of such a commitment cannot be determined. It is certain, however, that acceptance of such a commitment would be attended by grave risks, both military and political. While such a course might well serve to check Communist pressure in Korea and to discourage for the moment aggression elsewhere, it could scarcely provide the basis for a long-term policy in the Far East unless it were carried out on a scale that is thought to be impossible in the present state of American capabilities. In spite of these objections, it should be recognized that the pressure to initiate such a course exists and that the present policy for Formosa would not rule out such action.

In fact, the biggest unresolved element in the prob-

Associated Press on May 16, 1951, that to start a counter-offensive on the Chinese mainland would require six months of preparation after adequate equipment and supplies were made available in Formosa. An assumption that Chiang Kai-shek is ready and eager to take his legions to fall upon the Chinese Communists and is being restrained from doing so only by the interposition of the United States Seventh Fleet would be fallacious. It appears likely, of course, that if the present restrictions were removed the Nationalists would resume air and sea raids against the mainland. But it is believed that such attacks could produce no decisive results, and that their chief effect would be to intensify Chinese Communist hostility to their authors and drive the Chinese people, especially those suffering directly from the raids, into the arms of the Communists. Chiang Kai-shek could not expect with the present resources of the National Government to launch successfully an amphibious invasion of the mainland. There is nothing in Chiang's past record to suggest that he would embark on such an undertaking unless his venture were substantially underwritten by the United States or the United Nations or both.

lem of Formosa is the question of the ultimate direction in which policy will move. Much of the weight of decision in this matter will fall upon the American public. The current policy itself has been founded in great part on the American people's interpretation of what has been taking place in the Far East. It is public knowledge that the initial official reaction to these events represented a different judgment and pointed in a different direction. It is also clear that the actions of the Chinese Communists and the strains of the war in Korea have brought official judgment into ever closer conformity with public opinion.

The process by which public feeling and official action have been brought together on something like a common ground has been, however, one of stress and strain. It raised strong winds of political controversy and it rode roughshod over many important considerations. These considerations, some of which relate to the ultimate position of the United States in the Far East, others involve the position of the United States in the United Nations and among the free nations of the world, have not been disposed of. They have only been pushed aside for the time being.

Progress toward disposing of the problem of Formosa is temporarily in suspense. There are elements in American thinking that vigorously argue that the problem must be kept in a subordinate place. There are also elements that press for decisions that would come close to making Formosa and the National Government of China the hub of a Far Eastern policy. There are factors in the Far Eastern situation and factors in the international situation that can be referred to and be involved in support of either point of view. The actual course of events in the immediate future will certainly tend to weight the scales of judgment by calling for urgent, short-term decisions. Yet what will be the nature of these decisions is still the great question.

Nevertheless, it may be assumed that policy makers in addressing themselves to the problems of achieving short-range objectives will take account of the desirability that decisions which are made will not be inconsistent with the serving of long-range objectives. In regard to the latter, statesmen may be expected not to overlook considerations of the significance of an ultimately free China to the entire free world. China occupies a large and strategically situated segment of the earth's surface. Its hundreds of millions of people, with their heritage of sturdy individualism and habits of industry and thrift, have a potential capacity to contribute much, under favorable circumstances, to the common well-being and advancement of all mankind. This had been demonstrated by the richness of China's cultural gifts to surrounding peoples. A further important consideration is the value that would accrue from a restored trade between China, on the one hand, and Japan, Southeast Asia, and the Western World, on the other hand. Conversely, the stultification and perversion that the Chinese people have undergone under Communism, can do—and is already doing—incalculable harm to the peace-loving peoples of the world.

The main purpose of this study has been to assemble and arrange the facts that are relevant to an answer to the questions here raised, if and when it becomes necessary for the people and the Government of the United States to give an answer and to stand upon that answer.

The history of the Formosan problem is complex. Each step has been confused by controversy, and the logical progression has been obscured by strongly felt and vigorously expressed hopes and fears. It is believed that the mere sorting out of the facts of the situation, and the placing of them in some sort of perspective was and is an essential first step in laying the ground-work for future decision.

APPENDIXES

Geographical Place Names

The apparent multiplicity of names for the same geographical feature or place in Formosa, which is very confusing to the Westerner, arises from the fact that, in transcribing those names into Roman script, some Western writers or map makers have followed the standard Chinese pronunciation of the Chinese symbols (ideographs) with which the names are written; some, a southern Chinese pronunciation; and still others, the Japanese pronunciation. To the Chinese or the Japanese, however, inasmuch as the identity of a name is fixed by its written symbol or symbols, the diversities of pronunciation are of little consequence.

Each Chinese ideograph represents a simple idea or thing (for example, *swift, running, water*) and is read by the Chinese, but not necessarily by the Japanese, as a single-syllable sound. Most place names are of two syllables, though single-syllables and three-syllable names are not infrequent. The number of ideographs in a name corresponds of course to the number of syllables.

The Chinese written language is uniform through the length and breadth of the country, permitting intercommunication through the written word, but in the coastal provinces from Shanghai southward, where various distinct vernaculars are spoken, the pronunciation of the written symbols differs considerably from district to district, and even more from the standard or national language, which is the mother tongue of the population from the Yangtze valley northward. Some 15 centuries ago, the Japanese adopted the Chinese system of writing for the transcription of substantive words, but even in those cases where they borrowed the pronunciation along with the symbol, there is seldom any resemblance today between the way a Chinese and a Japanese respectively would pronounce the symbol.

When the Japanese occupied Formosa, they took over the Chinese place names as written, but they pronounced the names in their own way. Romanized texts and maps published during the period of the Japanese occupation, between 1895 and 1945, generally follow the Japanese pronunciation, whereas those published either before or after that period follow a Chinese pronunciation, usually that of the standard language, but sometimes that of a southern Chinese dialect. In the case of the name *Taiwan,* the standard Chinese and the Japanese pronunciations of the two ideographs representing "terrace" and "bay," with which the name is written, happen to be identical. However, the name of the capital city, *Taipei* ("terrace north"), in standard Chinese, becomes in Japanese pronunciation *Taihoku* and in Cantonese *T'oipak*. The Japanese sometimes, as in the naming of a new town or for sentimental reasons, applied purely Japanese names. Thus to the highest peak, known to Europeans as Mt. Morrison, they gave the name *Niitaka Yama* ("new high mountain"), in recognition of the fact that after the Japanese conquest this peak superseded Mt. Fuji as the highest in the Empire. The symbols for "new high mountain" are pronounced in Chinese *Hsinkaoshan,* and this is the name by which Mt. Morrison is generally known to the Chinese today.

A further cause of confusion is that in some cases there is also a European name. Thus, for instance, the island cluster in Formosa Straits, which we identify by the name *Pescadores,* is called *Penghutao* by the Chinese and *Bōkōtō* by the Japanese.

In the present text, the accepted European name will generally be used when there is one, and the Chinese and Japanese names will also be given where necessary for clear identification. When there is no European name, the standard Chinese form will generally be given. An exception will be made in the name of the principal northern seaport. *Keelung,* which, though it constitutes an unorthodox spelling of a southern pronunciation, has been firmly established. That name will therefore be used in preference to the standard Chinese, Chilung.

There is given below a list showing the Chinese and Japanese names, and, when there is one, the European name, of the geographical features and places in Formosa referred to in the text.

Chinese Name	Japanese Name	European Name
Chilung (Keelung)	Kiirun (Kiryū)	
Changhwa	Shōka	
Hsinchu	Shinchiku	
Hsinkaoshan (Yu)	Niitaka	Morrison, Mount
Hwalienkang	Karenkō	
Ilan	Giran	
Jih-yuehtan	Jitsugetsutan	Candidius, Lake
Kaohsiung	Takao	
Penghutao	Bōkōtō, Hōkōtō	Pescadores
Suao	Suo	
Tainan	Tainan	
Taipei	Taihoku	
Taiwan	Taiwan	Formosa
Tanshui, Tamsui	Tansui	
Tzukao	Tsugitaka	Sylvia, Mount

2.

Selected Bibliography

Ballantine, J. W. "I Lived on Formosa," *National Geographic Magazine,* Vol. 87 (January 1945), pp. 1-24.

Bate, H. MacClear. *Report from Formosa.* (New York: E. P. Dutton and Co., 1952), 290 pp.

Berrigan, D. "Should We Grab Formosa," *Saturday Evening Post,* Vol. 222 (Aug. 13, 1949), pp. 30+.

Davidson, J. W. *The Island of Formosa, Past and Present.* (London: Macmillan Co., 1903), 46 pp.

Dennett, Tyler. *Americans in Eastern Asia.* (New York: Macmillan Co., 1922), 725 pp.

Directory of Taiwan. (Taipei, Taiwan: China News and Publication Service, Ltd., 1951), 107 pp.

Fifield, R. H. "Formosa Acquires Strategic Value in China Crisis," *Foreign Policy Bulletin,* Vol. 28 (Mar. 4, 1949), pp. 3-4.

"Formosa in Transition," *The World Today,* Vol. 4 (May 1948), pp. 209-17.

Han Lih-wu. *Taiwan Today.* (Taipei, Taiwan: Hwa Kuo Publishing Co., 1950), 157 pp.

The Japan Year Book 1943-44. (Tokyo: Foreign Affairs Association of Japan, 1943), 1099 pp.

Kerr, G. H. "Formosa's Return to China," *Far Eastern Survey,* Vol. 16 (Oct. 15, 1947), pp. 205-08; (Nov. 5, 1947), pp. 224-26.

————. "Some Chinese Problems in Taiwan," *Far Eastern Survey,* Vol. 14 (Oct. 10, 1945), pp. 284-87.

————. "What Should United States Do in Formosa," *Foreign Policy Bulletin,* Vol. 29 (Dec. 23, 1949), pp. 2-3; (Dec. 30, 1949), pp. 2-3.

Kirjassoff, Alice Ballantine. "Formosa the Beautiful," *Na-*

tional Geographic Magazine, Vol. 37 (March 1920), pp. 246-92.

Ravenholt, Albert. "Formosa Today," *Foreign Affairs,* Vol. 30 (July 1952), pp. 612-24.

Rutter, Owen. *Through Formosa, An Account of Japan's Island Colony.* (New York: H. W. Wilson Co., 1924), 288 pp.

Takekoshi, Yosaburo. *Japanese Rule in Formosa.* (London: Green and Co., 1907), 342 pp.

U. S. Department of State. "Formosa," by Eugene H. Dooman, Hugh Borton and Cabot Coville, *Bulletin,* Vol. XII (June 3, 1945), pp. 1018-23.

U. S. Economic Cooperation Administration. Tenth, Eleventh, Twelfth, and Thirteenth Reports to Congress for quarters ending Sept. 30, 1950, Dec. 31, 1950, March 31, 1951, and June 30, 1951 (Washington: Government Printing Office, 1951).

U. S. Senate Appropriations Committee. *United States Aid to Formosa, Staff Report of the Special Subcommittee on Foreign Economic Cooperation of the Senate Appropriations Committee.* 82 Cong. 1 sess. (Washington: Government Printing Office, 1951), 8 pp.

Vosburg, F. G. "Poor Little Rich Island, Formosa," *National Geographic Magazine,* Vol. 97 (February 1950), pp. 139-76.

INDEX

Index